MOUNTAIN ODYSSEY

ONE MAN'S SUMMER IN THE CANADIAN ROCKIES

BRENT R. LEA

DRAWINGS BY GLEN BOLES
FRONT COVER PAINTING BY CECILIA LEA

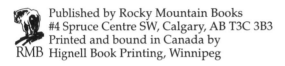

Published by Rocky Mountain Books
#4 Spruce Centre SW, Calgary, AB T3C 3B3
Printed and bound in Canada by
RMB Hignell Book Printing, Winnipeg

We acknowledge the financial support of the Government of
Canada through the Book Publishing Industry Development
Program (BPIDP) for our publishing activities.

National Library of Canada Cataloguing in Publication Data

Lea, Brent R. (Brent Roger), 1947-
  Mountain odyssey : one man's summer in the Canadian Rockies / Brent R.
Lea.

  Includes bibliographical references.
  ISBN 0-921102-99-2

  1. Lea, Brent R. (Brent Roger), 1947- --Journeys--Rocky Mountains,
Canadian (B.C. and Alta.)* 2. Rocky Mountains, Canadian (B.C. and
Alta.)--Description and travel.* I. Title.
FC219.L42 2002   917.1104'4   C2002-911107-2
F1090.L42 2002

TABLE OF CONTENTS

These writings are dedicated

with respect, to my wife,

Cecilia.

With her love and support,

I adventure!

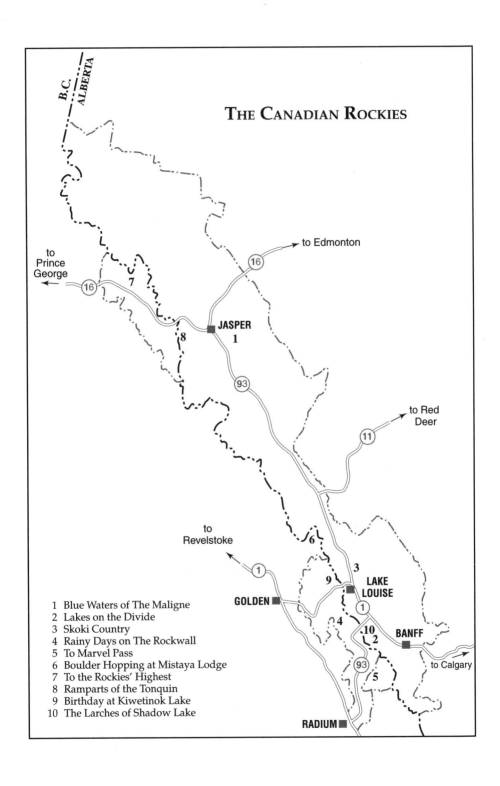

THE CANADIAN ROCKIES

B.C.
ALBERTA

to Edmonton

16

to
Prince
George

16 7

8 JASPER
1

93

to Red
Deer

11

to
Revelstoke

6

1 3

9 LAKE
LOUISE

GOLDEN 1

4

10 BANFF

2

to Calgary

93

5

RADIUM

1 Blue Waters of The Maligne
2 Lakes on the Divide
3 Skoki Country
4 Rainy Days on The Rockwall
5 To Marvel Pass
6 Boulder Hopping at Mistaya Lodge
7 To the Rockies' Highest
8 Ramparts of the Tonquin
9 Birthday at Kiwetinok Lake
10 The Larches of Shadow Lake

CHRONOLOGY

Blue Waters of the Maligne, June 22–26, 50 kilometres

Lakes on the Divide July 1–7, 50 kilometres

Skoki Country, July 8–14, 50 kilometres

Rainy Days on the Rockwall, July 15–18, 55 kilometres

To Marvel Pass, July 20–27, 70 kilometres

Boulder Hopping at Mistaya Lodge, August 4–9, 55 kilometres

Ramparts of the Tonquin, August 11–14, 50 kilometres

Birthday at Kiwetinok Lake, August 28–31, 40 kilometres

The Larches of Shadow Lake, Sept 18–21, 40 kilometres

DISCLAIMER

The author warrants all hiking distances and height elevations contained within these pages to be approximate. "About that time" and "Around about" are phrases that should accompany all historic dates. There are several excellent publications, some of which appear in the attached bibliography, that can offer the reader precise and completely accurate data.

I think myself fortunate amidst
the peace and quiet of Nature
Conrad Kain

INTRODUCTION

We all have dreams, and each of us has a special one, an important visionary idea that stands the test of time. A wish, a fantasy; call it what you may. It is something unique that we would *love* to accomplish before it's too late! It propels us along and keeps the candle glowing as we charge through our hectic life.

In the summer of 2001 I realized my long held vision—a summer spent hiking and exploring the trails of the Canadian Rockies. However, as the scope of my self–imposed challenge came into focus, I felt a certain apprehension and concern. The reason for those feelings was rooted in the fog of bewilderment that had shrouded my life for the past several months. Allow me to explain.

On a wintry day in early January 2000, I was notified by my doctor that I had contracted cancer. The following weeks were consumed with supporting tests to confirm its presence and in February, just before Valentine's Day, I underwent surgery at the Foothills Hospital in Calgary. In late March I began a comprehensive Chemotherapy and Radiation program at the Tom Baker Cancer facility—a program that lasted until early November. For that entire time, my life and my family's lives were in limbo; I worked very little, and my wife Cecilia and I derived no enjoyment from family outings and special occasions. We waited with baited breath throughout that long year, desperately hoping for a positive outcome.

So many questions ran through my mind during those interminable months. Why me? How long do I have? What can be done? Will the treatment work? What the hell am I going to do now? Of course there were no answers. The questions sapped my energy and resolve, and I gradually accepted the stark reality that there would be no definitive answers. The best course of action would be to simply adopt a "wait and see" attitude—an almost impossible task for me.

I have always needed a plan, a course of action; I simply must have order in my life. "Wait and see" does not work well for me. I had swerved off the road of life and was nose down in a deep ditch. I had lost my direction and confidence in some of life's basic guarantees. I needed to get back onto the road, and quickly. As I crouched down there in the gloomy depths of despair, with furtive eyes I searched the roadside apron and there appeared like an angel, my wife Cecilia. She was closing in on my location with a tow truck; a nurturing strength and unwavering love. With these devices she hooked on to my shattered soul and pulled me back onto the road. Fortified with a strong resolve, I accepted the new playing field. The road was now full of twists and turns, its surface marked with potholes. Still, it was a road and while I was unsure of this new terrain, I knew that I was on it and would have to work diligently and with purpose to discover its direction.

Of all the myriad questions that ran through my mind at the time, one always seemed to float to the surface of my brain pan and I decided to answer it as well and as fully as I possibly could. The question was: if you *really do* have a finite time ahead of you, what *are* you going to do with the rest of your life?

~

The quick and simple solution for me was to go hiking. All my life I had enjoyed being in the mountains. I felt that if I could still hike, I could prove to myself that all was well and fine. The trails, the passes and lakes would be the same, and my cancer just a bad dream. I would ramble the hills as I had in my youth, my treasured, healthy youth. But what if my health had been compromised, what if I no longer had the strength to climb to the alpine? I viewed my ability to hike as a barometer. At the time, hiking was the single most important thing I wanted to accomplish. "Wait and See" was not a viable option. I wanted to know if I could still do it.

And so it was that on a rainy day in early July 2000 I hiked up to Borgeau Lake in Banff National Park, and when I arrived, I continued on up past Harvey Lake to the pass, perhaps 300 metres higher and three kilometres farther along. I rested at the top well satisfied with my efforts. I still had it, I thought to myself, even with the exhaustive Chemotherapy treatments, I was still able to tough it out; and I was quietly pleased. I returned to the truck that evening more tired than I cared to admit, and began planning another, more ambitious hike for the following week.

The next week saw me on the Monarch Ramparts. I was hiking through country that the legendary Bill Peyto had called home almost a century ago. Over the years I had heard and read about Peyto and had developed a liking for his philosophy. His terse yet colourful way of explaining his love for the area struck a chord deep in my soul. While he had always been careful not to tell the Banff locals about the this precious land, he shared its beauty with his wife Emily, taking her up there many times over the years to see the lovely wildflowers and quiet mountain tarns. That day, it felt like my home as well and I enjoyed the mountains and the warm sunshine. I paid scant attention to the fact that I was perhaps a little slow, a little tired.

I felt the ghostly presence of Bill Peyto leaning on my shoulder that afternoon as I sought out the shade of a mountain larch. As the wind sighed through the branches I could hear that old pioneer's salty advice. "Don't you start goin' soft on me pardner," he opined. His blue eyes sparkled and his moustache twitched. "These mountains can heal ya. Trust me. You can do this. Why looky yonder on the Healy Meadows son; lookit all the damn fine scenery! Git yerself some backbone!" I was tired and let my mind drift across the rocky headland.

Ebenezer William Peyto wandered for many years in the Rockies as a park warden, trapper, guide and outfitter, and amateur geologist. He loved this country, even had a few cabins in the area. He had a 'misery in his guts' in later years and died from cancer at the Colonel Belcher Hospital in Calgary in 1943.

"Yeah, me too Bill," I thought wryly. I sat and watched the cloud shadows on the Monarch. "Ya know Bill, I've been here with my friends, my wife, my father, and my children over these last thirty–five years, and I love these passes, these meadows and lakes. I feel at home here. Why I used to ski right over there at

"Peyto assumes a wild and picturesque though somewhat tattered attire. A sombrero, with a rakish tilt to one side, a blue shirt set off by a white kerchief (which may have served civilisation for a napkin), and a buckskin coat with fringed border, add to his cowboy appearance. A heavy belt containing a row of cartridges, hunting knife and six-shooter, as well as the restless activity of his wicked blue eyes, give him an air of bravado. Part of this was affectation, to impress the tenderfoot, or the "dude", as he calls everyone who wears a collar."
Walter D. Wilcox, *The Rockies of Canada*, 1903. Page 119.

Sunshine when I was but a young sprout, used to fish these lakes around Simpson Pass. Hell, I almost drowned over there at Larix Lake, Bill, but that's a yarn for another time." I looked around and realized I'd been nattering away to myself. Bill was nowhere about but as I bent over to grab my pack, I was sure I smelled some old pipe smoke, wafting through the meadow.

I stood and continued up along the Rampart ridge. I began to realize that part of my heart, the dark and fearful part, had actually helped me to get up on that ridge; the dark part that had earlier whispered, "Hey buddy, maybe this cancer will steal you away from this wild and lonesome place. Maybe even this winter. Hell, this may be your last summer. Wouldn't you like to gaze down on the Healy Lakes just one more time?" And part of me thanked my black heart, but these dark thoughts, while they had propelled me up to the Ramparts, dissipated like the morning mists of a new day.

I hiked along the rocky ridge until it abutted the Monarch massif. Cutting down to the left through treeline larch, I found myself in residual snow on the shores of Eohippus Lake. A limestone fan of fallen rock ringed the near shore and I settled against a sun–warmed boulder to rest. It was about 4 pm and I still had a long day ahead of me. I sat and watched the ripples play across the lake and remembered the last time I had been there, 28 years ago, with Cecilia and my dog, Spook. Behind and above, some clattering stonefall shook me from my reverie and I squinted over my shoulder, hoping to see a mountain goat. It was not a billy goat after all. It was billy Peyto, moving nimbly across the rocky talus toward me.

"Ya can bust a leg doin' that Bill," I admonished.

He scowled, "I wuz mining and sinkin' shafts on this ridge when your granpappy was courtin' the ladies. Don't tell me how to mind m'self." He brought forth his pipe and fixed me with his icy blue eyes. "Lookin' a might done in there lad. Cancer takin' your spirit?" I admitted I was pretty tuckered. "Yeh, know the feeling." There was a pause. "Said earlier ya almost drowned at Larix," he snorted. "How the hell that come about?"

I told him about how I had gone fishing up at Larix Lake with a buddy when I was sixteen. "Found a canoe there Bill, back in the trees. We skidded it down to the shore and went out into the middle of the lake where the larger trout were rising to a fresh hatch."

I told him how ill prepared we were, no fishing net to bring the catch in over the gunwales, no life jackets, and no common sense. How both of us had fish on at the same moment, and we started hollering and whooping and flipped the canoe in a heartbeat. With our hiking boots on we sank like stones, but with the adrenaline in overdrive, we both shot back to the surface like corks. I told him how we spent the early evening pushing towards shore as the sun set over the peaks near Mount Assiniboine. We both had a tight grip on the canoe, we knew we could never swim to shore with our heavy boots on. We focused on a shoreline larch and watched as it gradually drew closer. Once on dry land, we secreted the canoe back in it's rightful hiding place and beat a hasty retreat to Sunshine Ski Village, six kilometres away, soaking wet and scared.

Bill just sat and smoked his pipe. After he'd taken it all in, he shook his head, climbed down off the rock and wandered over to the far shore. In an instant he became one with the larches and glacier lilies.

The rest of the afternoon was sunny and warm but the 23 kilometre–day played me out. When I got back to the truck at dusk, I was so very tired. The combination of Chemotherapy and Radiation treatments was taking its toll. I needed my rest to keep strong for the drug treatment; I realized I could not keep hiking and tiring myself this way.

As I aimed my truck down the service road to the distant Trans Canada highway, both my vision and my spirit became blurred with tears of frustration. However, I also recognized that I had tried and I had won—won the chance to see the Healy meadows again. And I think it was at that precise moment that I set my course; I now knew where my road led. I now knew the answer to the convoluted question of what to do with the remainder of my life if, indeed, we were measuring days. If God would just let me stay strong a little longer. I silently asked Him for one more healthy summer, and my request was granted.

~

For several years I had explored the idea of a long hiking challenge; to spend a large block of continuous time in the Rockies, and make it a kind of grand goodbye to the peaks. I, of course, would never give up visiting the mountains, but as the seasons moved along, I knew that I probably would not be able to venture too far into the backcountry.

As I drove my Greyhound bus along the highways over the years my mind was free to wander in pursuit of this dream. My original idea was to backpack from Waterton Park to Jasper town—an ambitious undertaking for someone who had done very little backpacking. On topographical maps I roughly figured out the route, which, except for an area between the Crowsnest Pass and the Elk Lakes, was amazingly straightforward, the entire area interconnected by a strong trail system. I planned food drops near the trail, drops that could be reached by road because I did not want to incur any flight expenses. And on and on I dreamed as the miles piled up on my bus and the years piled up on my body.

Gradually I realized this trip would probably not occur, and I felt a quiet uneasiness, perhaps even a little guilt. While I professed to love my mountains, it seemed I was unable to commit to them. What could be wrong? I thought maybe a less ambitious plan would provide the incentive. An abbreviated hiking trip took shape, a journey I began calling, "Shark to Shark, Taking a Bite out of the Wilderness." This hiking excursion would start from the Mount Shark trailhead south of Canmore, head north into the heart of Banff National Park, eventually coming around again to finish at the Mount Shark trailhead. Roughly circular, the route would include some of the best scenery the Rockies have to offer, and pass through seldom–visited areas within the park. However the hike did not encompass a large enough variety of our mountain scenery. It would miss a lot of beautiful areas in other National and Provincial Parks.

The miles and the time continued to roll along. I needed a push to get me going, and what a frightening push it turned out to be. The demonic spectre of a life–threatening disease was the catalyst I required. As I sat and received my chemical infusions at the Cancer Centre over the summer months of 2000, I developed a strategy. As the final details coalesced into a definite plan of action, I knew that I would have the heart and dedication to follow through.

The final plan came together during the early months of 2001. I decided to do several hikes in different parks, each trip lasting from five to eight days. The hiking season would be July and August, and I planned eight hikes that would fit into that time–frame. I used, as a reference, a guide book by Graeme Pole called

Classic Hikes in the Canadian Rockies. In addition to the hikes, I also planned to visit two backcountry facilities, Mistaya Lodge and Shadow Lake Lodge, and a trip to Jasper National Park to canoe on the tranquil green waters of Maligne Lake, the largest lake in the Canadian Rockies.

~

I approached my company with a request for a leave of absence, from June 15 to August 31 and after some deliberation, the request was granted. The next major hurdle was to enlist the help and support of Cecilia. I asked her to devise a nutritional menu for me and to act as a porter, bringing supplies to various trailheads on a weekly basis. Once I left my home in Cochrane, I did not want to return to civilization until the end of August. I wanted to feel completely immersed in the mountain mystique, to feel the presence of mountains about me every day. It would not seem fitting to come back home, to have a shower, to hear a telephone ring, or perhaps to catch up on the news on TV. I was beginning to look forward to spending the summer among the mountain peaks.

~

Our eldest daughter, Heather, gave us a dehydrator for Christmas, and Cecilia put it to good use. Over the spring months, she planned daily menus for me and dehydrated vegetables and fruits for my journey. These, in addition to oatmeal, porridge, cream of wheat, pasta, rice and lots of gorp (good old raisins and peanuts), comprised my diet while out on the trail. I knew I would miss certain foods like fresh veggies, seasonal fruits and berries, a good steak, french fries, and even Tim Horton's donuts. We decided the transition day, when I would meet Cecilia and collect my next hike's provisions, would be a good time to sample some of the delights denied to me while I was hiking along the trails.

While Cecilia was busy with the immense undertaking of constructing a proper diet, I applied for backcountry permits and arranged for campsite spots along the trails, made the required reservations and paid the obligatory fees. I joined a health club on a three–month membership to try to get into some kind of shape. This undertaking was only moderately successful. My job consumed much of the week, and with various other activities, there seemed little time to visit the gym.

I spent the months of April and May making sure I had the proper hiking necessities with which to enjoy the summer, and quietly monitoring my physical well being. Taking stock of myself, I felt I was in adequate shape. After all, it was just walking in the mountains: I wasn't going up Mount Everest! The Chemotherapy had ended the previous November; the debilitating effects of leucovorin running around inside my body chasing errant cancer cells like an obscene version of Pac–Man were now a distant memory. Still, I had little experience with carrying a load on a regular basis and I had a "trick" back. Two or three times a year, it would go out; vertebrae would nick an adjacent nerve, causing a spasm, which in turn would cause sharp pain for a couple of days. It would be hard to shoulder a pack under those conditions. My knees were 54 years old and I had not been kind to them over the years. However, while I felt my health had been compromised from the chemotherapy program I had received, I did feel strong enough to move forward with my plan.

I rooted around our dark and musty cellar, unearthing old hiking equipment and making a list of things to buy. While I had a couple of old backpacks, I thought perhaps I should treat myself to a new model. Advances in technology allowed me to acquire a pack specifically designed for my back. To have a proper, ergonomically designed pack seemed well worth the expense. I bought the pack, an Arc'teryx Bora 65 at Mountain Equipment Co–op, and had it professionally adjusted by their staff for my back and projected payload. It had a 420d Ripstorm nylon coating—whatever the hell that was—as well as an anatomic compression moulded back panel. Boy, I was sure I would need that! The *piece d' resistance* had to be the V–stay suspension system with integrated composite load transfer rods. And let's not forget the highly touted nickel–plated zipper sliders. Lots of adjustable straps for shoulder configuration and top–load capabilities, an aggressive style of hip belt, lumbar pads for the lower back attached with velcro straps, and the list went on and on. I thought back to my first pack, an old Trapper Nelson which, though simply constructed, had served me well during those formative hiking years.

My other expensive purchase was my hiking boots. I had been fortunate with my feet over the years, in that I seldom had trouble fitting boots to them. The Asolo's I purchased were no exception. Over the course of the summer, not once did I have a blister or hot spot, in fact I quite often thought of them as my bedroom slippers. At the end of a day, I would continue to wear them around the camp and into the evening—they were that comfortable.

I made a few other purchases to fine tune my ensemble. Heather had some great tips including things like a polyproplene tee shirt to wick away sweat, special wool socks which would also help keep my feet dry, and a platypus, which is a plastic receptacle that fits in the top of the pack and holds two litres of water. The water could be sucked up through a plastic tube clipped to a shoulder strap and it turned out to be a great help. As one climbed a hill, it was far more accessible than a water bottle. I also bought two aluminum, adjustable walking sticks that were immensely helpful when going downhill with a heavy load. A Primus stove, lightweight and inexpensive, propane/butane fuel canisters, some cooking pots, and other sundry items rounded out my purchases. I already owned, what was referred to as a summer–weight sleeping bag, which served me adequately, a camp mat, and enough hiking clothes, including shorts and a fleece jacket. I required one further item, and that was a good tent. I eventually bought one, though I found out later it was a second from an obscure sports store. On inspection, some of the tent material had been improperly cut, and some of the stitching seemed suspect. Still, it appeared serviceable and was moderately priced. It stood up well against the vagaries of summer weather, rain and hail, hot sun or wind, and I was happy with its performance.

During May and early June, I walked the river trails near my home with my new pack, carrying 55 pounds for the first time in my life. After some initial pack restructuring, it started to feel quite comfortable on my back. I went for an eight kilometre walk one day and on returning home, I judged everything to be completely satisfactory.

June 15 soon appeared on the calendar, and Cecilia and I took off for our canoe trip on Maligne Lake in Jasper National Park. We were looking forward to this adventure and planned to use the experience to see how the dehydrated food would work out. I viewed it as a shakedown cruise for my forthcoming summer activities.

Blue Waters of the Maligne

Were we novices? For sure! First timers? You bet! We were neophytes of the first order and if someone had asked us about our destination that day our reply would have been less than knowledgeable.

Cecilia and I arrived at Maligne Lake early on the morning of June 22nd for good reason. Simply put, we were new to the game. We wanted to get underway before any tourists or fellow canoeists could watch and critique our inept attempts at loading a canoe and venturing out onto the lake. There was even an outside chance that we might roll the canoe over before clearing Curly Phillips boathouse. I rehearsed in my mind the swim to the dock, spluttering and dog–paddling, while holding, between my teeth, the yellow nylon cord that was tied to the front or, excuse me, the *bow* of the canoe.

We had spent some time the previous day at the Parks Canada Information Centre in Jasper, reserving camping spots on the shore of the lake and trying to ask intelligent questions about what we could expect out there in terms of distance, paddling hours, and weather conditions. The Parks staff attendant quietly assured us that it was not really a major undertaking, it was in fact pretty straightforward. "Maligne Lake is 22 kilometres long and has two camping sites, here and here." She penciled the spots on our map. "Fisherman's Cove is right here, 12 kilometres or so, and Coronet campground is down at the end, just about here, maybe another ten klicks, there about. Ah, you'll be fine!" She folded the map and, with a special smile she reserved for hapless souls, showed us to the door.

We went back to camp to organize our equipment for the five–day trip. I went over again in my mind what she had said, back at the info centre. We'd be alright, were her words, but little did she know. We had used this canoe perhaps four times in our life! All of them on Lake Windermere, a small lake in the Columbia Valley, south of Radium, B.C. and, compared to Maligne, warm as a bathtub. Our longest paddle on that lake had been to Indian Beach, a gruelling three kilometres! We knew virtually nothing about canoeing, had no idea what a J–stroke was. We were as green as our Ram X–15 canoe.

Now here we were, ready to shove off onto the flat mirrored surface of Maligne Lake, the largest body of water in the Canadian Rockies! The calm morning induced a false level of confidence, but was appreciated, none the less. Our gear was stowed between the gunwales, across the bottom of the canoe to keep the load as low as possible. The last thing to go in the canoe was our 30–pound Border Collie, Spirit. As Spirit tried to settle herself amongst the duffle, the canoe shifted alarmingly from starboard to port and I felt that if Cecilia and I could not dump the canoe, perhaps good ole' Spirit would do it for us!

The canoe scraped against the gravel bottom as I manoeuvred it into deeper water sending Spirit into a paroxysm of anxiety. She bailed out for the green grass of shore. She was not "The Captains Dog" after all. She was in fact, a certified sheep-herding Border Collie and sheep do not live out on the water!

Moreover, she was not a swimmer, and as she made a beeline for the shoreline, only her be whiskered muzzle showed above the lake surface. We headed back to shore to retrieve the errant mutt and finally coaxed her back into the boat with a death–grip on her collar. True to her benign nature she settled obediently onto the duffle and we pointed our canoe to the distant Samson Narrows.

Hugging the shoreline and twisting in and out of little coves and bays we gradually relaxed and became comfortable with this new mode of transport. Spirit enjoyed watching the shoreline drift by and in less than two hours we put ashore at Four–Mile Creek to stretch our legs.

We floated down the lake and in time, came to Samson Narrows. From the air, these narrows might appear as the slender part of an hourglass. So far we had not seen any other canoeists or kayakers. We were on our own and it felt quite peaceful and remote. While most of us in canoes and kayaks hug the shoreline, tour boats travel up and down the centre of the lake. They are quite removed from the canoe route except at Samson Narrows. Here the channel is but scant metres across and so extra caution is required by all waterway travellers.

The tour launches come from facilities at the head of the lake, referred to as "Home Bay." They are usually full of sightseers and ply the waters of Maligne Lake from nine am until evening. They are not as disruptive to people in canoes as one might expect; the wake generated by their passing the only concern. The Captains are courteous and throttle down as they pass smaller craft. In addition there is a resident park warden who monitors the situation from his outboard. As a result, everything seems to run quite smoothly.

Our campsite, at Fisherman's Cove was just beyond the Narrows and we arrived shortly after noon. It was a well planned camp nestled in a small bay and when we arrived, we were the only ones there, except for a porcupine that scurried away on our approach. We beached the canoe and tied the dog, in case she thought the porky was just another toy to play with, then searched for a tent site in the pines. There were eight tent pads and metal food storage lockers. The lockers were about six cubic feet in size; large enough to store food and spare equipment safely away from foraging bears and chewing porcupines.

As the afternoon wore on, more canoeists came into camp; some from Home Bay while others came in from the south end of the lake, down by Coronet Creek. We moved along the shoreline and tried our luck at fishing, using an old fibreglass rod I'd found in our basement and some cheap monofilament line. I had a couple of lures that had been with me for over thirty–five years, when I was a kid and had figured myself to be a mighty fisherman. Over the course of the afternoon Cecilia and I passed the fishing pole back and forth and caught and released three or four brookies and two nice rainbows, each one weighing about three pounds! Back in camp that evening, we met some fellow campers and fishermen and enjoyed the camaraderie of like–minded fellow "voyageurs."

~

The next day was cool and showery and we spent the day exploring the shoreline of the Samson Narrows on foot and by canoe. We caught another six or eight fish that day, their tug on the line as they hit the lure and their tail–slapping splashes across the green waters of the bay taking me back in time to my youth. I now remembered how much I had enjoyed this pastime with my buddies.

The park warden came into camp during the afternoon to check for camp registrations and fishing licences. A member of the RCMP, the policing force in Jasper, accompanied him. At the time park wardens were negotiating with the federal government for the right to carry firearms. As the policing and enforcement service in Canada's national parks, they felt they had valid reasons for being armed. The federal government did not share their point of view. While this ongoing concern was being addressed, the park wardens were using the RCMP to help them enforce national park policies. The RCMP constable I chatted with in camp was "happy as a clam" with this arrangement. He told me he would far rather patrol the back country by horse or boat than police our crowded highways riding a Chevy!

~

The following morning we packed the canoe for the trip down to the southeast end of the lake. The early morning mist that shrouded the surface of the lake quickly burned off as the sun rose into the clear blue sky. Presently we arrived at Spirit Island, the picturesque destination of the tour boats and we went ashore. It was too early in the day for the sightseeing cruisers, so we were rewarded with solitude. No throbbing diesel engines, clicking cameras and gaily–clad sightseers.

After a brief visit ashore we eased back into our canoe and slowly paddled into the next part of the lake, heading in a southeasterly direction, while hugging the western shoreline. Here we felt as if we had come upon a different lake. The streams that drain from the glaciers above carry vast amounts of silt and glacial till into the lake. The fine particles of rock flour remain suspended in the water resulting in the most intense hues of aquamarine and turquoise. It was, to us, absolutely stunning. The lake's complexion was vastly different from the appearance of the lake on the north side of the Narrows. Added to this vibrant colour was the lush green growth that came right down to the water's edge. Rich mosses and shoreline bushes seemed to grow right out of the water. The part of the lake we had traversed before had a gravel shoreline perhaps three or four metres wide. Constant wave action generated by the tour boats lapping the shoreline had stripped the fertile cover from the lake's edge.

We paddled slowly through this surreal landscape in the shadow of Mount Paul, a high buttress to our left that overlooked the lake and was part of the Queen Elizabeth Range. We rounded Porcupine Point and entered a sheltered bay on the silent wings we called paddles and came within six metres of an immense bull moose stripping willow leaves from a lakeside bush. The noise from his grinding teeth overshadowed our stealthy approach and we sat still as a log on the transparent surface of the bay, waiting for him to take notice. He casually hooked some branches away and glanced over his withers in our direction. His quiet gaze seemed to imply, "So what's the big deal? I knew you were there all along!" We sat and watched for ten minutes before moving along; the shale–covered lake bottom three metres below, reflecting the shadow of the canoe.

At Spindly Creek, we disembarked for lunch. I set a bottle of Jackson–Triggs white wine into the creek to chill, and we ambled about the forest getting the kinks out of our backs. On the warm grass near the bubbling brook, I read from Mary T. S. Schäffer's book, *A Hunter of Peace*. She is credited with being the first European to see Chaba Imne, now known as Maligne Lake, in 1908. She and her outfitters followed the trails of early explorers from Lake Louise to Nigel Pass before venturing into the uncharted wilderness in search of this fabled lake. With interest, I read of her astonishment and disgust at the garbage and refuse left behind on the trails by various outfitting parties that had moved through these mountain valleys and passes all those years ago. Schäffer contended that these exploration parties should take better care of this sublime wilderness and clean up after themselves. One suggestion she made was to fill cans and bottles with pebbles and sink them in lakes and rivers—an out of sight, out of mind philosophy. While we know better than that now, Cecilia and I did precisely that as a tribute, if you will, to Mary Schäffer. Having drained the contents of the Jackson–Triggs, I peeled the label off and put it away in our refuse bag along with the cork, filled the bottle with pebbles, and once out from shore a few metres, I dropped it into 50 metres of water. We looked sheepishly at each other, and convinced ourselves that no one would ever be able to retrieve the bottle and procure our fingerprints! It didn't seem quite as bad, for example, as the hundreds of empty oxygen cylinders that have been left behind, over time, on the south col of Everest! On some obscure level, we paid homage to an old pioneer.

We paddled on down the lake in a gathering wind that soon had whitecaps dancing on the surface—a new and disquieting experience. We were just becoming comfortable with our paddling; how would we now handle waves and wind? We watched with fascination as a bald eagle flew along the shore with us for over an hour. He would fly ahead, then alight on a dead branch. As we approached, he would languidly spread his wings and do a circle or two above our heads and move farther down the lake, imploring us to follow. We would catch up to him, waiting patiently on a snag and the sequence would begin again. This happened four or five times and it looked for all the world as if he was guiding us in the right direction to the camp at Coronet Creek. Later on, as we came within sight of camp, we watched as he ascended into the thermals above the lake and vanished.

We came ashore on a gravel outwash shortly before camp where Mary Vaux creek debouched into Maligne Lake to stretch our legs and explore. The creeks at this end of the Lake drain from glaciers and snowfields on Mount Mary Vaux, Coronet Mountain and from the vast Brazeau Icefield. Circling through the gravel and sand around the creek, we came upon some cat prints we took to be cougar; they were larger than the outstretched palm of my hand.

Back aboard, we headed north around a point of land where the wind coming down the lake did its' best to beach us. Freezing water splashed into the canoe and we were very relieved to turn the headland and paddle downwind. Within a few minutes we reached the secluded bay near the end of the lake and landed near the Coronet campground. It was wild and remote down there; the only way in is by boat. There is no lakeshore trail and no access routes come in from neighbouring valleys. We were over 20 kilometres from habitation. Again, we were the first ones at camp. We spent the afternoon setting up our tent, dozing in the warm sun and perusing Mary Schäffer's chronicles. Reading her description of this fantastic wilderness and being right in her footsteps filled us with the same passions she felt. Mary Schäffer and her horse party were right there, ninety years ago. How that feeds the imagination!

Gradually the camp began to fill up, and we greeted some of the folks with whom we had shared camp back at Fisherman's Cove. Most expressed surprise that we had decamped so early. We explained that for us its a grand experience to rise in the cool dawn of a new day and get moving in the wonderful mountain grandeur. We joked and kibbitzed over dinner with our fellow canoeists and then paraded down to the lakeshore to take in the dazzling orange brilliance of the setting sun on the Monkhead, a limestone buttress that rises above the end of the lake. The lake was shaded in nightfall; the fir and spruce trees ringing the bay, the darkest shades of blue and purple.

~

During the night a cold front moved through the valley and heavy rain pelted the tent fabric. I rose at first light to make some coffee. No one was about and the trees were still dripping–wet from the storm. With warm brew in hand, I threaded my way through the underbrush to the lakeshore in time to see some Harlequin ducks. These rare birds are beautifully coloured and not always easy to spot. They nest in the area at this time of year and we had been advised in Jasper to watch for them.

Across the lake, above Warren Creek, the clouds started to climb and disperse from the valley floor. I could see fresh snow on the slopes of the peaks. It was time to leave. After an early breakfast we loaded the canoe for the return trip to Fisherman's Cove.

We wanted to paddle up the opposite shoreline, the northeast side, but were hesitant to cross the lake right there. No one was up in camp, and if we flipped, I was not sure we would be able to signal our distress back to a sleepy camp. Instead we did the prudent thing and swung around the shoreline, which probably took us an extra hour and possibly saved our necks. At the extreme end of the lake, opposite Warren Creek, a strong breeze came up out of nowhere, and we began a fight with a quartering wind. The canoe rocked and Spirit became increasingly agitated with the motion and cold spray. I threatened her with the paddle and she jammed herself under a thwart where she became an inert rock in the bottom of the boat, which was just what we needed. We tried to keep the canoe nosed into the waves and gradually we came into the protection of the forest on the lee side of the lake.

We stroked up the shore heading in a northwesterly direction and taking in the frozen views of Mount Mary Vaux and Llysfran Peak to the southwest. These 10,000–foot peaks harbour a large hanging glacier that looked spectacular in the morning sunshine. On an avalanche fan below Mount Unwin, we spied two cow moose foraging on the fresh undergrowth and watched them through our binoculars.

As we approached Spirit Island, we crossed to the other shore to avoid the tourists. With perfect timing, and at the narrowest spot possible, we came abruptly upon a motor launch that had not yet seen us. The skipper immediately throttled down, but the churning wake was unnerving in the confined space and the wave motion bounced back to us from the shallow bottom. We took it broadside, but we were only ten metres from shore, and everything worked out fine. Cecilia and I effected our stony squint like the seasoned *courier d' bois* we had become and Spirit, still sulking from the paddle, glanced over at the boat with a malevolent stare. Her mood did not improve as, just two minutes later, a hailstorm came dancing and hissing across the lake. We put in to shore and tried to get in under some trees, but ended up getting pretty wet as did our dog. She was beginning to really hate the water!

The shower moved on down the lake and an hour later we were in camp at Fisherman's Cove. The evening was sombre and damp, but we had a warm and cheery fire, which we shared with some of the other campers. Two fishermen came into camp and cooked up some wonderful Brook trout that they passed around. Succulent with firm, orange tinted flesh, cooked with onions in butter, the fish feast was the high point of the evening.

~

It rained all night and the next morning was cold and grey. The cloud ceiling was only 300 metres above the slate–grey surface of the lake. We pushed off for Home Bay and immediately ran into a stiff headwind as we paddled through the Narrows. This was the last day of our trip and we resolutely applied ourselves to the task at hand, facing into the wind and rain and keeping our heads down.

As miserable as it felt, we sat with our unspoken thoughts and kept paddling. We both knew that this had been a very special trip. We had learned some canoeing skills, caught some fish, made some friends, and seen some truly spectacular scenery. As we approached Home Bay, the sun came out from under the heavy clouds and by the time we came ashore, we were dry and warm and full of smiles!

LAKES ON THE DIVIDE

The early rays of a new day filtered in through the windows of my home. I paced about with a final cup of coffee warming my hands, hoping I had remembered everything. With luck and good fortune, I would not be returning to the comfort of home for about 60 days. A final check in the back of the truck revealed my pack, poles, boots and camera. We were off, my odyssey about to commence.

Cecilia drove me out to the Sunshine Parking lot, 20 kilometres west of Banff, and in the fresh morning air, I shouldered my pack, kissed her goodbye, and stepped onto the trail to Healy Pass. It was a blue–sky morning and as I ascended the trail, I looked back to see her wave a final time. I was now on my own, and a seemingly long journey lay ahead. I would be hiking virtually every day for the next two months; my fifty–pound pack a constant companion.

This hike, my first of the season, would take seven days, and cover about 50 kilometres from the Sunshine parking lot to Vermilion Pass, near Storm Mountain. The route climbed over three passes: Healy, Whistling, and Gibbon, and I hoped to see twelve backcountry lakes during the week.

Walking alone quietly that morning, I felt the set of the pack on my shoulders and enjoyed the sunshine as it filtered down through the roof of the forest. Breathing slowly and shallowly, I reminded myself that this was, and would be, the order of the day for the next couple of months. It was probably best to approach this undertaking in bite–sized mouthfuls, just take it one week at a time, or if need be one day at a time.

I hiked along with Healy Creek chattering beside me. The trail I was walking on had a long history. It had been used for centuries by various Aboriginal tribes, most notably the Shuswap. In 1841, they guided Sir George Simpson, who was then the governor of the Hudson's Bay Company, through these mountain ranges. Healy Creek, which drains from the pass of the same name, was named for Joe Healy, a prospector who had come north from Montana in the 1860s. I crossed the creek three kilometres into the hike and rested by the bridge for a few moments. I ate a snack while two hikers, out for the day, passed with a wave.

After drinking some water, I headed back to the trail. Climbing past the Healy Creek campground and up into the alpine I caught my first glimpse of the Monarch Ramparts through the larch trees. Once into the relatively open sub–alpine meadows, I was somewhat surprised to see how little snow remained from the past winter. After all, it was only the first of July. I had been here at the same time in other years when the snow blanketed the pass in early summer, with the glacier lilies pushing gallantly through the snow cover in search of the warm sun. There had been however, very little snow over the previous winter, so I guessed this was to be expected.

The mountains had been enduring below–average precipitation for the past few years. As I hiked throughout the summer of 2001 I saw evidence of the dryness in the decreased water levels in several lakes, especially those that drained underground. Cascades were diminished because of shallow snowpack in the alpine and in some areas trees had died because the poor snowpack offered limited insulation against the vagaries of winter weather.

After filling my water bottle, I ascended the two remaining kilometres to Healy Pass. With beautiful white, fluffy clouds floating over the Monarch, and wildflowers such as spring beauty and anemone nodding their heads in the passing breeze, I felt the first stirrings of something that would remain with me for the rest of the summer. It was a feeling of peacefulness, a tangible sense of being in the right place, at the right time.

Near the pass, which lies at 2330 metres, I met two hikers, Nathan and Laura, out from Canmore for a day of hiking. We exchanged pleasantries, and discussed the history of the area, particularly the local wanderings of Bill Peyto. I mentioned that Peyto had trapped and mined in this locale, even had a cabin around here somewhere, a cabin he referred to as the Bookrest. Nathan agreed, and as Laura took photos of the wildflowers, he questioned me on my knowledge of the area, where I was from, etc. After a time, he judged me to be someone with whom he could share a secret.

Now, we both already knew that Bill Peyto was, to put it mildly, uncomfortable around people; he preferred his own company. Any cabins he built were hard to locate as he took great pains to keep them out of public view. The Bookrest proved to be such a cabin. I knew that there were some people in the parks service who were aware of the location of this particular cabin. There is for instance, at the Lake Louise Visitor Centre, a coat on display said to belong to Bill Peyto, and said to have been recovered from the Bookrest Cabin. On this warm and sunny afternoon, Nathan told me where it was. He and Laura had discovered it on their own after three summer seasons of searching. Back in Canmore, he found several others knew of its location. Those who know, he told me, do not travel there in the winter; they don't want others following ski tracks to the door. He seemed to feel we were now brothers in a conspiracy and swore me to secrecy before we parted.

I contoured along the escarpment below the pass pleased with my newly acquired knowledge. Snatches of an old poem by Jim Deegan floated through my mind.

On Simpson Pass, atop the Divide,
among the yellow tamarack
stands a cabin in a meadow,
a lone prospectors shack.

Weathering in the elements,
abandoned in the vale,
a sod–roofed fortress, built
beside an old packtrail.

The cabin tells a story
of a miner and his claim:
of a pioneer in the wilderness,
Bill Peyto was his name.

The log octagonal building,
its welcome mat of sharpened spikes
leaves a person with a feeling
old Bill had his dislikes.

In my library at home, I have a good picture of Bill Peyto, with his horses, in front of the Bookrest Cabin. I made the decision that sometime soon, though not on this trip, I would search for the cabin. I smiled as I imagined ole' Bill looking down on me from some lofty domicile watching as I traipsed hither and yon in search of his hidden abode.

With Columbian ground squirrels chirping in the trailside grass, I crested out on Healy Pass just after noon hour and there I rested for 30 minutes, looking at the wildflowers, and thinking how, in a few short weeks, grizzlies would be arriving to enjoy the bountiful spring greenery. I left the pass in a gathering wind, feeling strong and happy. I had climbed my first pass, with a 50–pound pack, and I felt none the worse for wear. As I dropped into the valley, I looked over to the base of Haiduk Peak, to see Talc and Scarab lakes, tucked in under the imposing limestone buttress and still crusted over with late–winter ice.

The farther I descended, the warmer the day became, and when I reached Egypt Lake campground early in the afternoon, it was hot and calm. With 13 kilometres under my boots, my hips started to imply that I was carrying too much weight. I took the pack off to search for a tent site. It was a long weekend and very busy. I counted 11 tents already in place. I finally chose a site, set up the tent, and took my foodsack with me to find the local "bear–hang," which I located near the food preparation area, some 200 metres away.

These bear–hangs, as I call them, are food storage areas provided by Parks Canada and available at every backcountry campsite. A bear–hang is an improvised way of keeping foodstuffs and other odorous material suspended above the forest floor out of reach of animals such as squirrels, porcupines or bears.

A bear–hang consists of a length of cable strung between two trees spaced about ten metres apart that have been de–limbed to a height of about eight metres. Each end of the cable is secured to the tree about seven metres above the ground. From this cable hang six or eight lighter cables on pulleys. A camper simply attaches their foodsack or backpack by means of a carabiner to a convenient loop on the cable and hoists them up out of reach of bears. The bottom end of the cable is secured to an eyebolt in a nearby tree. After hanging my food out of harm's way, I returned to the tentsite to organize my camp.

During the evening, with the lowering sun shooting brilliant light across the landscape I sat in the meadow carpeted with glacier lilies, caught up on my journal and watched some late arrivals stagger in. My bright yellow tent, in the evening sun, gave off a reflective glare so intense that I could not look directly at it. There were at least 30 people at Egypt Lake that evening, yet all was still and quiet, most of the campers keeping to themselves. With the sun setting and the air cooling the bugs came out for some liquid refreshment. They were a hardy breed, and did not respond in an appropriate fashion when sprayed with OFF.

The warden came by to say hello and chitchat. She was a seasonal warden, and moved throughout the summer to various districts within the Parks. Though there was heavy cloud–cover building in the west, she assured me that the forecast was for continued stable, clear sunny weather. Toward dark, I retired. As the creek burbled behind the tent, and the mosquitoes whined on the tent netting, I reflected that the first of 62 days was now behind me. Already I felt immersed in the mountain environment, already, I felt at peace.

~

I spent the next two days exploring the area around the Egypt Lake campground. I woke early the first morning to bright sunlight on the east face of Pharaoh Peak, and wandered over to the common cooking area to have my breakfast. This area, which I was to become familiar with at other camps over the summer, served a variety of purposes. All food consumed in the campground is cooked and eaten there, to prevent tempting food smells from permeating the sleeping area. An feature of the common kitchen is that it draws campers together to exchange information and ideas. It was always at such gatherings that I would hear of a bear sighting, or a tough stream crossing, and where I would meet people from different regions.

The common kitchen area at Egypt Lake campground is located very close to the bear–hang and food sacks, and the only drawback seemed to be its lack of proximity to a water source. I found this to be a concern at many of the backcountry sites I visited over the summer. This particular morning, most hikers were heading out, as it was the end of the long weekend. I found that my hike would probably be a solitary venture as no one I spoke with was headed for the route I had chosen.

After washing up the dishes and putting some food in my fanny pack, I struck off up Pharaoh Creek under blue skies and warm temperatures. Talc Lake, which is located just over the border in British Columbia, is about four kilometres from the campground. Initially the trail appeared rarely used and followed the creek through a narrow defile perhaps 30 metres wide. The stream murmured beside me and a breeze swept down from Red Earth Pass. I kept a watchful eye for bear signs as I knew I was moving quietly. About one kilometre along the trail I saw a large bear print in the trailside mud. I felt that it was reasonably fresh but decided the owner of that particular paw had crossed the trail rather than travelled along it.

This was only my second day out and I was not completely comfortable as a solo hiker. It is always safer to hike with someone or in a group and while I felt reasonably confident, I was not a born woodsman. I could interpret a sign incorrectly, or miss an important wilderness clue. After seeing the pawprint I knew I still wanted to continue and so, for the next while, I hollered and blew my whistle making my presence known to any animal within earshot.

Just before Red Earth Pass, an obscure trail branched south and ascended into a fine larch meadow. Here the trail became more pronounced as it turned into an old cart track. I realized it was the old tote road that served the mine at Talc Lake between 1927 and 1943. During those years talc, used in the manufacture of talcum powder and for explosives, was mined here and carted down out of these alpine basins to a railhead at Massive, on the shores of the Bow River. While the cart track was now quite overgrown, it was still three metres wide and delineated by large rocks that had been moved from the track to create a smoother roadbed.

While I had seen evidence of activities of this nature in other locales, and in different mountain ranges, this was my first experience in a National Park. I thought about the early miners living far from the nearest town, scratching and clawing into the talus slopes in search of raw mineral deposits, then extracting the ore, loading it onto mules and two wheel carts and transporting it 11 kilometres down the Pharaoh Creek valley, along the marshy borders of the sub–alpine creek and on into the deep forest. A bridge was constructed over the Red Earth Creek and the journey continued for another 12 kilometres to a bridge over the Bow River at a CPR siding known as Massive. From there the ore was loaded on trains for export. It was hard for me to understand the time, the work and the fiscal gains of such an undertaking.

As I mulled these thoughts over in my mind I ascended into the cirque holding Talc Lake, and quite suddenly popped out of the trees onto the lakeshore. Immediately my eyes focused on the large waterfall across the lake, a cascade that tumbled from a ridge perhaps a hundred metres above the water. I stood by a larch and took in the scene. The slight breeze playing across the lake surface caused the late winter ice along the shore to shift and crackle.

I was surprised to spot two people on the shore, off to my right, as I had thought I was alone. We chatted briefly. They had been at the lake for perhaps 30 minutes and were going to continue on up to a snow–choked col (a narrow steep passageway between two rocky ridges) northeast of the lake. This route would eventually lead them past Mummy Lake and back to Egypt Lake. They asked if I would like to join them. It was very tempting, however, as I had just arrived, I wanted to drink in the scenery for a bit. I also wanted to visit the old mine site, if I could find it. I bid them a safe journey and watched them step off through the larches.

As there was no trail in the area I guiltily trampled wildflowers with every step. They were always underfoot in untold billions it seemed, their yellow heads contrasting with the lush spring grasses. Glacier lilies carpeted the immediate environs of the lakeshore; after these showy flowers have gone to seed the grizzlies will move in and excavate the meadows to eat the nutrient–rich roots and bulbs.

I sat and enjoyed this peaceful area for about a half–hour, just resting in the warm sun and scanning the adjacent talus fans. I noticed a tote road on the opposite side of the lake and walked over to investigate. I boulder hopped the outlet stream and immediately came upon some old cabin foundations, four of them, each about 12 x 20 feet. Their footings, now just so many rotting logs, had been shored up with flat rocks from the lakeshore. I found an old dinner gong, a triangular shaped affair that would call the faithful at mealtime. Moving on, I discovered three artfully–contrived, stone baking ovens built into the hillside, and farther on, some pits lined with tin remnants I thought perhaps had been used as cold–storage areas.

The first recorded visit to Talc Lake was by Colonel Robert O'Hara, in 1895. He was the first European to find a soapy talc powder in the vicinity of Red Earth Pass. In 1917, Bill Peyto staked a claim here and, in 1927, sold it to the National Talc Company. They in turn, sold it to Western Talc Holdings. From there it went to Wartime Metal Corporation which operated it for two years under the Wartime Measures Act in 1943. Again Deegan's poem came to mind and danced across the cirque:

The clanging ring of horsebells
echoed from Borgeau
as Bill Peyto climbed the packtrail
from the town of Banff below.

Six kicking ornery packhorses
tied tail to tail to lead;
a cougar–hound named 'Lightning'
panting 'longside old Bill's steed.

He was heading for his talc mine,
the other side of Pharaoh Pass,
and his horses were right eager
to feed on alpine grass.

Reloading the packs at the cabin,
tied with diamond hitches,
his only conversation was,
"Whoa there, you sons a bitches."

I looked up at the tote road, still covered in residual snow and noticed some large tracks traversing the slope. I climbed up on the bench and on approaching them noticed some telltale white hair on a young larch. A goat had passed by, its hoof tracks now sun–dished from the warming rays. I was about 40 metres above the lake and sat down to rest. I would go no farther this day. With a grand view down the valley of Pharaoh Creek to distant Copper Mountain, I sat and observed and absently wondered why Pharaoh Creek comes from Red Earth Pass, why Red Earth Creek flows from Ball

Pass and Shadow Lake? I looked down on the mine workings and tried to imagine men, tough as rawhide, operating in this austere environment. I stayed there for about 45 minutes before descending to the lakeshore. The air was heating up under the clear sky and I slowly wandered on down into the Pharaoh Creek drainage arriving back at my tent in mid–afternoon. I had been gone about five hours and had travelled about ten kilometres.

After an refreshing wash, I rested by my tent and was visited by a group from Stettler, Alberta. The leader, Hank, was a high school teacher in that town and had brought three fellow teachers along. They had also set out for Talc Lake that morning. They had seen me up ahead, but decided to turn back at the bear print that I had observed on the trail. Hank felt it was a little too fresh, and there were two novice hikers in his party.

Over at the Egypt Lake cabin, I met a couple, Rolf and Marquita, from Switzerland. We got to talking and it turned out Marquita had worked at the Quality Bakery in Invermere the previous year. I had lived in the Windermere Valley for a time and that bakery was one of my old stomping grounds. They seemed like good folks, but I got the feeling they enjoyed their private time and so I moved along.

Back at the tent, I spent the evening killing bugs and reading. A man and his son from Florida occupied the tentsite next to mine. We conversed a bit as the evening light flooded the land. He told me that he spent a great amount of time in the Canadian Rockies every summer. His son Robbie was hiking with him this season in an attempt to lose 20 pounds in order to join the navy. At twilight, with pink and orange clouds floating quietly over the Pharaoh Peaks, I turned in for the night.

~

The following day, I hiked up to some lakes that I had never visited before. I was aware of their location—high in the cirques under the Pharaoh Peaks—but on previous trips into this area there had never seemed enough time to visit them. The lakes— Pharaoh, Black Rock, and Sphinx were within a few kilometres of my camp.

I breakfasted with the group from Stettler, which was outbound that day. They seemed to feel I was in need of more food and, as they were leaving anyway, Hank decided to give me the extra food they would no longer need. I acquired some power bars from them, and about four pounds of GORP. Hank also gave me a spare fuel canister, a cartridge which, by happy coincidence, fitted my stove.

The day was clear and hot and I did not get going until mid–morning. But within the hour I was on the shore of Pharaoh Lake, tucked in a cirque with larches ringing the shoreline. The trail had been quite steep but had afforded splendid views of Red Earth Pass and the distant Monarch Peak, which dominated the skyline above the Healy Meadows. After crossing Pharaoh's outlet stream on some sketchy, water logged timbers, I ascended through a mature larch forest to Black Rock Lake, arriving about 40 minutes later.

This lake gets its name from a huge black towering buttress on its southern shore, and still had some residual ice on the surface. I skirted the right–hand shoreline to a talus fan at the end of the lake. This talus slope was comprised of rocky debris that had fallen from the cliff face above, a natural feature of erosion in the Rocky Mountains. I rested for 30 minutes on a huge chunk of limestone, taking in the warm sun and lovely views to distant Healy Pass. The trail to this lake was quite overgrown and evidently seldom used. Some timber cut along the trail looked very old and it made me think of the Boundary Commission, which had passed this way in 1922. Could it have been they who had originally cut this trail?

From charming Black Rock Lake I half–heartedly ascended to another distant cirque, this one containing the small tarn, Sphinx Lake. The trail was hardly discernable and I had read that the tarn was really small and of little scenic value. As the day was getting considerably hotter, bushwhacking quickly lost its appeal and after about 20 minutes I gave up and headed back to Black Rock.

Another notable feature in this area were the old "tree blazes" that I observed from time to time. These tree blazes provided an effective way for travellers to follow a route through the forest when the actual tread marks on the ground were hard to see, especially during the winter months. The blazes were made with a hatchet or axe which was used to strip a piece of bark from the tree perhaps a foot long, exposing the rich yellow wood fibre beneath. The marks would act as "flagging" for travellers trying to make their way through unknown territory. This was indeed, a very old trail. I slowly meandered back down to the campground at Egypt, arriving mid afternoon. The next day I would be packing up and leaving, heading toward Whistling Pass.

~

At noon the next day I was sitting on Whistling Pass with a refreshing breeze blowing across the narrow defile, admiring the view of Haiduk Lake below. So far, the day had been grand, though very hot. Within five minutes of leaving camp that morning, I had begun a long hot ascent along the cliffs to the west of Egypt Lake and had arrived in the meadows above Scar'ab Lake quite tired and soaked in sweat. The persistent mosquitos had been atrocious in the damp moss, precluding a lengthy stopover so I had continued on, the vagrant wafting of cooling air from the pass pulling me onward.

It was very early in the season so there were no flowers at this height, but the late winter snow provided a pleasing foreground for my pictures. The immediate surroundings held many "photo ops", and I took pleasure in the solitude as I rested there, feeling quite alone, but not lonely. I sat in quiet contemplation and pondered the reasons for the Egyptian names that had been applied in this region. I knew the Interprovincial Boundary Commission had travelled through here in 1922, under the direction of A. O. Wheeler, a land surveyor and past president of the Alpine Club of Canada. What had been their motivation to attach names such as Pharaoh, Sphinx, Mummy, Scarab, and Egypt? There is some speculation that one of the surveyors in Wheeler's party who had an interest in Egyptian history, suggested these names. One of the lakes, when viewed from the top of Pharaoh Peak can apparently look like a shroud–wrapped Mummy, while a lake directly below the peak has the shape of a scarab, which is an Egyptian beetle. Haiduk, on the other hand, is not an Egyptian word at all, but rather a Polish phrase for "lively."

I wasn't in a hurry to shoulder my pack and head down, as the scenery afforded from this lofty perch held me spellbound. The day was yet young, the temperature was soaring in the valley below and, I had been informed by other hikers, the bugs at my next camp were a venerable force to be reckoned with! However, after two hours, I felt ready to move on.

As I left the top and started to descend the snowy slope, I met an older couple accompanied by a younger pair coming up from Shadow Lake. It was early in the afternoon and they were not quite halfway into an ambitious 20–kilometre circuit. They looked strong and keen, and after brief greetings, I hiked on down toward Haiduk Lake. On the lakeshore, in windless conditions, my thermometer registered 30°C. The emerging flies and mosquitoes filled my mouth as I tried to breathe and got in my eyes. I did not linger long but continued on slowly, down to the Ball Pass campground.

I arrived in the late afternoon to find some fellow hikers swatting bugs and moving aimlessly about in a hopeless attempt to avoid them. The stream from Ball Pass rejuvenated me and I enjoyed a complete wash. Everyone cooked dinner outside their tents swathed in fleece jackets, toques and mittens to keep the mosquitos from gorging on their exposed flesh. I spent the evening inside my tent, away from the tormenting bugs, reading and writing in my journal.

~

Ball Creek flowed quietly beside my tent as the soft light of an early dawn stole into the valley. It was very early, perhaps five am, and the constant whine of mosquitoes reminded me that I would have to "suit up" to go outside. The day was to be an easy one for me, just five kilometres down to the Shadow Lake campground. I lingered in my bag, hoping the bugs would die of old age, but no such luck. I dressed in the tent, donning mitts and toque and headed over to the kitchen area for breakfast. It seemed all of us there were suffering from the debilitating effects of the bugs and, as a consequence, the breakfast became a very rushed affair. With minimal conversation, we applied ourselves to the task of filling our collective faces, then scurried back to the tents to pack.

I got underway quickly and tracked off down the open meadow in the mid–morning heat. The bugs and the heat were beginning to take a toll on my calm demeanour. I had little energy and was thankful the day would not be a long one. As I walked, some high cirrus clouds blew in from the west and blotted out the gorgeous sky. In less than two hours, I arrived at Shadow Lake followed by a strong wind. After taking a long look at Mount Ball with its richly defined ice couloirs and corniced snowcap, I hiked to the lodge a kilometre away and set my pack down. Out of curiosity, I entered the lodge, and there, drinking tea, was the foursome I had met the previous day up on Whistling Pass. They told me that they had indeed finished the long trek yesterday, though it had taken longer than anticipated. After a sound night's sleep, however, they felt none the worse for wear. They were an intriguing group. The older couple, Cameron and Sylvie were in their late sixties and hailed from South Africa. Their son Neil and his wife Judy were from Vancouver. We chatted for a while, and then I left to set up my tent in the campground about 300 metres farther on down the trail.

I had the campground to myself. It was very peaceful, graced by some large, well–spaced spruce trees. The meadow and stream was visible through their great, sweeping branches. I went for water and was surprised to see a tap attached to a hose that wound like a snake through the trees, evidently coming from the lodge. The bonus was that as the hose was black plastic, and the sun was very warm, the hose produced warm water at an ideal temperature in which to wash.

An hour later, I went back to the lake for photos and found my South African buddies. Neil was deeply involved in photographing the immediate flora, as was I. We struck up a conversation and began to share a common bond. Chatting came easily to us. We went back to the lodge near dinnertime and Judy "stood me to a beer." I was surprised and elated to get that frosty can in my mitt and spent little time draining the contents. Warm water and cold beer in the same day! Things were definitely looking up! We nattered on for a while longer, sitting on the deck of Shadow Lake Lodge. I learned they were going into Skoki the next week. I was going there as well, this time with Cecilia. I agreed to stop by the lodge at Skoki for a quick visit.

As I reclined on the front porch, appealing aromas from the kitchen wafted by my nose and I was compelled to go back to my bear–hang for some dehydrated vegetarian chilli. It was very quiet and lonesome there; the sombre forest my only companion. I reflected on the lodge, as Cecilia and I had reservations there in September. She would love it in there; the cabins were very modern log affairs, with views of the sweeping meadowland in front.

Back at the tent, I turned in early. My back was becoming decidedly gnarly and I thought it needed to be stretched out for a bit. The pack today was nowhere near as comfortable on my back as it should have been. By now, it should have felt as if it belonged there, but I felt like I had fought it all day. Tomorrow I would pack the contents differently and hopefully achieve a more comfortable fit.

~

On the morning of July 6, I tumbled out of the tent into the chilly dawn; intent on catching an early sun as it warmed the castellated ridges of Mount Ball. It was a quiet, clear morning and I knew that I would be rewarded with some wonderful photo opportunities. I hustled into my fleece and boots. In an all–fired hurry to get out, I tripped over the fly and sprawled out onto the damp grass, tucked into a shoulder roll and came up on my knees. Exiting the tent was an ongoing vexation. As far as I know, no one has devised an easy way to egress a small tent; you just tumble out, stumble and fumble around, grunt and groan a bit, maybe even trip and turn an ankle. It just never seems to work out gracefully. For me anyway. I kicked away the cursed nylon fabric, jumped up and looked furtively about, thankful that I was alone in the camp.

Through the trees, I could see Mount Ball blazing in her morning attire of tangerine. I knew I was too late to get over to the lake, so I satisfied myself with a meadow picture; the grasses wet with dew and the dark spruce against the vivid orange a delightful contrast. It was not until far later in the summer that I found out Colin, my friend of almost 40 years, had succumbed to the ravages of cancer on that pretty day. July 6. I will always remember the vibrant, golden light on Mount Ball, a fitting tribute. The peak was a bright orb that morning, lighting the new trail on which my friend had embarked.

Members of the Palliser Expedition had named Mount Ball when they travelled up the Bow Valley in 1858. The expedition was sponsored by the British Empire, so many notable features along their route had been named for prominent Britons. Mount Ball had been named for John Ball who received recognition for his political support of Palliser's voyage to western Canada.

I was on the trail to Gibbon Pass very early after breakfast. In the cabins, not a creature was stirring, not even a mouse. I reflected that when in a warm, snug cabin, one sometimes misses the best moments of a mountain morning. Is it not far better to freeze your parts off in a tent, waiting for the first grey hint of dawn, and then jump up and fall sprawling through the tent door?

I ascended through the forest on a good, albeit steep trail into the alpine, keeping watch for the first larches. They are always a good indicator that one is about to enter the sub–alpine and that shortly the views will improve. I was the first hiker on the trail that day. I knew this because I was constantly breaking through gossamer cobwebs that crisscrossed the path.

As I approached Gibbon Pass, I blew a few short bursts on my whistle to let the neighbourhood know about my impending arrival. I popped out of the trees onto the plateau rather quickly. The sightlines were good and just as I left the trees, I glimpsed a grey shape bolt through the larches, seemingly at a dead run. Fragmentary thoughts went flying about in my head. Bear, was the first thought, then I remembered Pole's book which had mentioned that this was prime goat country. Whatever the creature, it was angling away from me. Still, the ol' heart was pounding, both from altitude gained and adrenaline. I was not wearing my eyeglasses, so I just stood there and tried to blink the sweat from my eyes. Goat, bear; maybe a bear, for cripe's sake. What the hell *is* it? Canters like a goat, stiff in the rear legs, like a bear maybe? Within seconds the adrenaline rush was over. It continued veering away and I decided it was a goat. It hit the talus fan under an outlier of Storm Mountain at a gallop and was off and up the scree in a heartbeat; only an agile goat could pull that one off!

I meandered across the plateau of Gibbon Pass for over an hour. It was very green and quiet, and a gentle breeze kept the mosquitoes in the damp moss. Looking to the south I could see my old friend, Mount Assiniboine in the far, hazy–blue distance. About three weeks from now I'll be hiking in the shadow of that lofty pinnacle, I thought to myself. I contoured down to the Lower Twin Lake, my lunch stop for the day, and sat by the outlet in warm sunshine enjoying the waterfall that sluiced down into the lake from the eastern flank of Storm Mountain. I heard voices and soon my South African friends emerged from the forest. They were such a happy group, and I took pleasure in their infectious cheerfulness. We shared the lunch spot and then they were off; they still had about ten kilometres ahead of them while I had only two kilometres to hike to my next campsite.

I reached my destination, Upper Twin Lake about an hour later. After setting up my tent and inspecting the immediate area, I hung my foodsack from the bear–hang. So far, I was the only one around and I wasn't sure how to fill the afternoon. Ridge scrambling on Storm Mountain was one option, but crossing the crumbling detritus off trail and by myself was not very safe. I had a lot of energy, having travelled barely seven kilometres, and part of me felt like continuing on to the highway, some eight kilometres away. There was no sense, of course, as Cecilia would not be expecting me until tomorrow, so I fussed through the hot, sunny afternoon—doing some wash, reorganizing my pack, and reading. It was very peaceful.

At dusk, two hikers came in, dusty, hot and tired. This was their first backpacking trip in the mountains. Matt and Randy hailed from Regina and were active birders. We ate our dinner together and it was a fun and informative time for me. I was introduced to the world of birding. It was amusing to watch them take a bite of food, then, while chewing, raise their binoculars to watch a rosy finch in a nearby bush, or to spy upon some other avian mystery farther out in the meadow. Together, later in the evening, we walked the lakeshore to watch some Barrow's Goldeneyes cruising on the still lake. I hit the sack at dark; it was completely quiet, their tent far removed from my own site, which was three metres from the lakeshore. I drifted off with pleasant thoughts of seeing my wife on the next day.

I was shaken awake in the dark of the night by what seemed like a giant rockslide crashing off the buttress at the end of the lake. In my groggy state of mind, it felt like it lasted at least a minute, and what in incredible roar! I could hear boulders pounding into the lake surface. I was camped about 200 metres from the end of the lake, not nearly far enough away, I mused. My active imagination saw chunks of shattered limestone screaming like shrapnel through the forest, shredding tree bark and tent nylon. I lay for several minutes, sniffing the air for sulphurous brimstone, and finally drifted off into a fitful slumber.

~

I decamped early on another picture–perfect, cloudless morning. What could be finer than rambling in the alpine at first light? Today I was heading to the highway above Vista Lake, to see Cecilia and later on, hopefully to enjoy some great food. Arnica Lake was just incredible as the first rays of the sun highlighted the mists above the water. I continued on down into the Vermilion Burn of 1968. At the time this fire was raging through Kootenay National

Park, Cecilia and I were living just west of Calgary. We watched with fascination the incredible orange and blood–red sunsets for two weeks as the smoke filled the western sky and the forest was consumed in the blistering inferno. Cecilia and I drove out on the 1A highway one day, to get a closer look. The Trans Canada highway was closed because helicopters and planes were using the road as a landing tarmac to refuel the fire–fighting equipment and resupply the crews. The Banff townsite, only 20 kilometres away, was prepared to be evacuated as ashes blew across the roofs and swirled along the streets. The lodgepole forest that sprung up after the fire is now about 25 years old and the trees over 20 feet high.

It was very windy that day and the few standing dead trees, sometimes referred to as "widow makers", moaned forlornly and swayed ominously as I passed beneath. It seemed they were so tired of standing and wanted only to lie down with all the rest of their friends.

Later on I rested by a chuckling stream and soaked my hot feet; my feet were my vehicle to future discovery—I needed to take care of them. The final push up from Vista Lake to the road was filled with memories of the past few days. My first hike was now complete, and already I was looking forward to the next one, into Skoki, this time, and I would have the company of my wife. I topped out shortly after noon, just as she pulled in with the truck. I was thirsty and happy, her smiles and kisses were like cool wine and brought laughter to my sunburned face.

The verses in this chapter are from the poem Prospector of Talc Mountain by Jim Deegan published in *Timberline Tales*. Revised edition, 1994. Coyote Books, Waterton Park, AB. ISBN 0-9692457-8-5. All rights reserved.

Skoki Country

Man, what a drag. What a tough way to begin a wilderness trek! Cecilia and I scraped one hot, dusty boot in front of the other as we laboriously ascended the gravelled track that had in years past led to the historic Temple Lodge. Thousands of old red and white Brewster ski buses used to groan up this twisty old road, but the expansion of the ski area at Lake Louise rendered them extinct. Now *we* were the ones groaning up the old track and the sun's heat was about to render *us* extinct!

It was close to noon on July 8, and that blistering orb shone from directly above effectively negating any vestige of shade from the surrounding forest. We had begun our hike a little later than we had intended and were now paying a heavy price. There were four kilometres of road ahead of us with an elevation gain of about 300 metres. Thoughts of cooling streams in the alpine kept us moving along. It seemed like such a brutal start to what was sure to be an exquisite and picturesque backcountry adventure.

We had awakened that morning to the soft sound of rain tapping on our truck roof as we lay camped in the forest at Johnston Canyon. The early grey light filtered into the truck bed and I had been excited and eager to roll out and get going on my next trip. My partner however, was not so easily roused from her slumber. But, she gradually came alive when the smell of coffee wafted through the camp, and soon began grousing about the hour and the rain.

However, the shower soon passed and a clear sky and hot sun emerged. After a fortifying breakfast of bacon, eggs, hash browns, coffee, kiwi fruit and Black Forest cake, we jumped in the truck and drove the 20 kilometres to the trailhead. We stopped briefly in Lake Louise to buy some serious bug repellent and mosquito headnets and then headed over to the Information Centre to check on the trail into Skoki. If there were any concerns— trail conditions or wildlife problems, the folks there would be able to offer helpful advice. Instead they provided us with a five–day forecast of stable weather and above average temperatures, and wished us a safe and pleasant journey.

With Cecilia for company, I was looking forward to an exciting ramble through some gorgeous country in the eastern ranges of the Rocky Mountains. Our journey would be a 60–kilometre circuit that would take us seven days to complete. Our route would take us past Halfway Hut to Boulder Pass, past Ptarmigan Lake and Baker Lake to Cotton Grass Pass and then down to the Red Deer Lakes. From the broad meadowland near these lakes, we would travel up through Jones Pass to the Skoki Lodge area and explore the shores of Merlin and Castilleja lakes. We would leave the valley by way of the Skoki Lakes, go up and over Packers Pass, and descend to the truck in the Bow Valley. We hoped to see over a dozen backcountry lakes and would climb over four different passes.

As we trudged along the dusty old road that day, I thought about the restful beauty that lay beyond. We finally crossed the last ski run and moved into the cool shade of the forest.

We soon came to what used to be a log–bridged crossing of Corral Creek. The bridge had been replaced with treated timbers and was no longer as picturesque as it had been. Views began to unfold around us and we stopped there for about a half–hour, if just to take pleasure in the rich, blue sky and the soft, white, fluffy clouds that came sailing over above us from the mountains along the Continental Divide. We laid on our backs and let the sun–warmed mountain sedges dry our sweat soaked T–shirts, before hefting our packs for the last kilometre to our campsite at Hidden Lake.

We got to the campground and set up our tent before going down to the crystal–clear creek flowing from Hidden Lake, for a wash and refreshing drink. Initially, we had the area to ourselves, but presently two brothers moved into the camp. We had spoken with them on the trail as we were coming in. One brother had been very talkative and animated in his gestures, but his sibling was the opposite and had stood back in the trees, his sunglasses and army fatigue hat hiding his facial features. It seemed he was incapable of both movement and speech. The sociable one told us that they were heading over to a campsite some 15 kilometres beyond ours at Hidden Lake. We surmised that they were strong and committed hikers because their trek that day would be over 20 kilometres long. It was now late in the afternoon and they still had a long way to go. And so we were not surprised to see them move off to the side of our camp and start to open up their tent. They certainly had an ambitious hike planned that would carry them into a remote, far northeast corner of Banff Park. Few people travel back there; they expected to be by themselves and would be gone for almost three weeks. Their packs, they told us weighed 80 pounds. However, they seemed to be prepared for whatever nature was about to throw at them. Both had what appeared to be army–issue camo pants and vests, belt knives and maps in packets strapped to their thighs, heavy, paratrooper style boots, binoculars around their necks and hatchets on their hips. They were an intriguing pair and bore slight resemblance to the rest of us out there with our lightweight equipment and colourful accessories.

Later, as we were preparing dinner, the talkative one appeared through the bush at our tent site. It seemed both of them had some aversion to established trails. I concluded that he had a decidedly stealthy way of moving through the woods. In his army surplus attire and that big "frog–sticker" of a knife strapped to his thigh, "Rambo," as we had dubbed him opened the conversation with "Say, I'm wonderin' if ya wanna make a trade?" Behind him I could see his 6–foot brother standing still as death and just as noisy, still wearing his shades. I looked over at my wife. My ever–active imagination took over and I became somewhat suspicious of this man's intentions. "Is it his *brother* he wants to trade, and if so, what's he think *I've* got to trade?" As my eyes darted about, looking for a weapon, I stood up, and fixed him with a beady eyed squint. "What's on your mind?" Scrunched up in his hand, I was relieved to see an innocuous looking bug shirt. "How 'bout I trade you this for a garbage bag? It's an extra one I got and I don't need it!" Now I thought that was a good bargain and I asked him why he needed a plastic bag? He informed me that he did not tolerate the established campsites in the park, of which this was one. He preferred the random camping that the parks offered in the more remote regions. In those areas, one could wander at will, as there were few designated trails and chop wood for fires, both for warmth and to get rid of garbage. "An' camp wherever I damn well please, near the crick, back in the trees, whatever turns m'crank!" He went on to say that as they had not yet made it into the random camping area, he was unable to burn his refuse and would need the plastic bag to carry with him until he could start a fire. He, of course, turned out to be a sincere wilderness trekker, enjoying the simple pleasures of the backcountry and honourable to a fault. He was not about to ask for anything back there—not even a garbage bag—without offering something in return. Honest values that exist in all of us emerge in the backcountry, yet back in "civilization", we sometimes hide these traits as we are so concerned with appearing vulnerable. I met this man months later at his job in Calgary and paid him for the bug shirt. I asked him how he had fared on his journey. He told me the trip had worked out well but the heat had been incredible. "Didn't hardly see nobody, the only animals we seen was squirrels."

After dinner, Cecilia and I wandered the two kilometres up to Hidden Lake as the sun slid down below the peaks. It was an enchanting evening, the meadows flooded with strong light from the lowering sun as it peeked out from under the cloud cover atop the Divide. Behind us, a waterfall cascaded down the flanks of Mount Richardson and into Hidden Lake. As the sun lay across the snowy cornices of Ptarmigan Peak, I was reminded of a poem by John Porter that I used to know by heart called "The Legend of Halfway Hut." As we moved across the ridge above the lake, I recited what I could remember. It was great fun; we were in the exact spot mentioned in the poem and I hollered out to the limestone arena,

Down from Ptarmigan Peak with a terrible shriek
and trailing vermilion flames
on his fluorescent skis, Gadner roars through the trees
leading Paley and both of the Daems.

The wind from their schuss bends the tops of the spruce
and startles the snows from the height,
and their yodels resound with a fantastic sound
as they hurtle along through the night.
To the Halfway they come, with their packs filled with rum,
at the doorway they kick off their skis.
Soon the fire is lit, and round the table they sit
and there they relax at their ease.

All the night long, there are snatches of song
and the clinking of glass upon glass
while the poker chips click and the playing cards flick
and phantasmal fortunes amass.

And on and on it goes. The evening mood seemed spectral as we rambled about the environs that had inspired the poem. Upon returning to our yellow tent, it was time for bed.

~

I got up before the sun, the damp coolness of another clear day a blessing. I knew that as the morning advanced, the temperature would soar. I grabbed the Canon from the tent and went down to the meadowland around Halfway Hut. It was completely calm, the only sound the distant chirping of a Columbian ground squirrel. I found a grassy hummock and sat to watch the morning sun slowly come into the glen. Across the valley, above the hut, the sun glittered and sparkled among the icy ridges and glaciers in the Valley of the Ten Peaks and along Mounts Victoria and Lefroy. It looked as if a diamond tiara had been placed upon these noble summits of the Continental Divide. The dark foreground needed some sun for purposes of photography, so I sat and waited and thought about the interesting history and folklore that surrounded Halfway Hut.

It had been built of sturdy logs in 1931, a stopover for skiers staying at Skoki Lodge. In those days, skiers left from the train depot at Lake Louise and the 20–kilometre ski trip up to the lodge was too arduous for some to accomplish in one day. Guests who stayed at both the hut and Skoki Lodge during those years were entertained with tales of the ghosts who supposedly inhabit the old refuge. The apparitions are reputed to be skiers who died in avalanches. The first victim was Dr. Edwin Paley, a lodge guest at Skoki. One afternoon in April 1933, he was skiing by himself on nearby Fossil Mountain and was swept away by a slide. A few years later, two brothers were killed by an avalanche while skiing in the Duchesnay Basin, over by Lake O'Hara. In 1945, Herman Gadner, an Austrian, was buried under snow in the Richardson bowl, up above Hidden Lake. As the poem goes...

When these two appeared, Herman Gadner cheered
as he poured them a nebulous rum,
"Now, the number is right, we play poker to–night,
by God, lads, I'm glad that you've come..."

Many well–known locals from Banff swear that the hut is indeed haunted, including notables such as Cliff White, Lizzie Rummel, and Ray Lagace who tells a fascinating story of coming up on Halfway Hut one winter night and seeing a candle burning on the window ledge. Happy for some company, he kicked off his skis and went inside. All was black and cold, no fire in the stove, no warm coffee. In the bleakness, Ray began muttering to himself about "seein' things." He went to the window ledge and there was the candle, warm to the touch and still dripping down the peeled logs, looking for all the world as if it had just been snuffed out!

If you're skiing by day past the old Halfway,
you may think it an ordinary sight,
for deserted it lies; but you'll rub your eyes
if you travel that trail by night!

After two hours, I was rewarded with the sun's caress on the old weathered logs, and took some photos before returning to the tent. We enjoyed a quiet morning meal, then packed up and started for Boulder Pass. Organizing my backpack was now getting much easier, everything had it's own niche, and it went together the same way every morning. My sleeping bag went in first, jammed into the bottom, then my "stuff sac," which held such sundry items as vitamins, toothbrush, medical kit, extra shirt, shorts and socks, down vest, toque and spare film. I would hammer this to one side to make room for the cooking pot, which also contained my stove, matches and spoon. I placed my fleece, rain gear, and wool gloves on top with a fuel canister on either side. The draw cord cinched everything in. The tent and sleeping mat rested on top of the pack. One side pocket held lunch for the day, the other one held a bug shirt, head net, insect repellent and my bear–hang rope. My camera was cinched to the front of my chest while the pack hip belt held my knife and bear spray.

When we arrived at Boulder Pass it was very warm, however a slight breeze was wafting about and so we rested there for 30 minutes. We were in no hurry; our camp for that night lay only five kilometres farther, on the shores of Baker Lake. Our guidebook informed us that it was, in mid summer, "the buggiest place in the Rockies." That's a very impressive statement, and if it was true, we weren't anxious to hurry on down to verify its accuracy. With distant views of Mount St. Bride and Mount Douglas, peaks that stood above the Baker Creek valley, we contoured around the north shore of Ptarmigan Lake, and slowly moved on down the escarpment toward Baker Lake.

The shoreline of Baker was alive with bugs; the sandy soil apparently a perfect habitat for their proliferation. It was windless and the heat down here was staggering. We dropped our packs and fished out the bug dope, donned our rain pants, bug shirts and head nets, gloves and toques, and marched the remaining kilometre to the campground. This campground proved to be the biggest disappointment of the summer, though at the time, we were glad to have arrived. We threw our packs down on the dusty ground, shook out and erected the tent, then jumped in all hot, sweaty and discouraged.

Once inside, away from the voracious mosquitos, we grinned at each other and calmed down. They of the "probing proboscis" whined by the untold millions around the tent and formed great clusters on the mosquito netting. We closed our eyes and the whine of the bugs sounded as if we were camped beside a four–lane highway. There were three other tents dispersed throughout the campground, occupied by hikers trying to dodge the insect onslaught.

Toward evening, we suited up and ventured forth to prepare our dinner. This is a very old campground, and has seen perhaps 70 years of use. We couldn't help but wonder why the parks service had not closed this site years ago and allow the vegetation to regenerate. There was no groundcover whatsoever, and the dusty trail to the bear–hang was two feet deep in places, worn down from many years of use. Gnarly roots of spruce and fir wound like serpents through the camping area, exposed by countless boots and hooves. The three remaining wooden cook tables were very weather beaten, and all the wooden stumps for sitting on had rotted away over the years. The "biffies" were an utter disgrace; old, grey, unprotected wood, gnawed by porcupines covered a latrine pit of the most disgusting odour. The wooden platform held no toilet seat, just a rough hole cut out by a handsaw. It was obvious the outhouse had not been cleaned in a long time. There was dirt, pine needles, and other refuse piled in the corners. The door sagged from one hinge; a bootlace had replaced the other hinge. Of course, there was no toilet paper. We had been told by Parks Canada to bring our own.

I reflected now, that I had paid $70.00 for a season's park pass for the truck, and another $10.00 to reserve this trip. In addition, Cecilia and I had each paid $42.00 for seasonal backcountry permits. With the recent federal government budget cutbacks, it was becoming increasingly difficult for the administrators of these mountain parks to provide and maintain an adequate level of service. In this particular camp, we were uncomfortable with the unkempt appearance and sanitary conditions and secretly envied "Rambo", out in the random camping part of the park, no doubt enjoying more pristine and natural surroundings.

We cooked our dinner by the lakeshore as the sun started its downward slide across the sky. We must have eaten a thousand mosquitos that invaded our pasta dish. Thunderheads were building in the eastern sky above Baker Creek and we heard the distant rumble of thunder. Though the air was cooling, the bugs continued their war on us and we retreated to the safety of the tent as the evening sun lit the distant thunderheads. It seemed a shame to hide in the tent ignoring the beauty of the area, but neither of us could abide these diabolical winged warriors. As we lay atop our bags, a common loon serenaded us from the glassy lake surface and the brief, gentle sound of a passing shower lulled us to sleep.

~

The morning of July 10 provided some outstanding reflections on Baker Lake under a crystal clear cerulean sky. Because of the mosquito problem, we decided to forget about breakfast. I put on my bug shirt and packed outside, while Cecilia put her pack together in the safety of the tent. It was another fantastic morning. We were packed and ready to go by the early hour of 7 am.

Tilted and Brachiopod Lakes are two small tarns about three kilometres to the south of Baker lake. After some deliberation, we decided to take the short side trip rather than starting immediately into our day–hike to the next campground. The picturesque ponds occupy some shallow depressions in the sub–alpine meadows and are well worth visiting. In 1911, John Porter, apparently the first European to see and describe these lakes, offered names that were not accepted, for whatever reasons, by our Dominion Government. He called Tilted Lake, Aquilegia, for the Columbine flower, while the other lake, Brachiopod, he called Pinnacle, for a large, triangular rock that rises above the surface, about 20 metres from shore.

Cecilia and I had been to Brachiopod Lake once before, in 1970 and we remembered being intrigued by the angular monolith projecting from its surface, an anomaly we had not seen before in our travels. Beyond this lake lies a splendid ridge offering expansive views to the south and east over the valley of Baker Creek, which flows 400 metres below.

We left our packs in the campground and ambled across the lower slopes of Mount Brachiopod and were at the lakelets in under an hour. We had hoped to find a clear stream to drink from along the way but were unable to, so we returned to Baker Lake, filtered some water and went to reclaim to our packs. "Satan's minions" hovered above the camp, darkening the sky, or so it seemed, crawling over our packs and flying at our faces with voracious intensity. They were absolutely atrocious, and though we were hungry, we threw our packs on and with hurried and harried goodbyes to our fellow campers, fled from the camp and headed out on the trail to Red Deer Lakes.

Within two kilometres we broke out of the forest and into the meadows of Cotton Grass Pass, a scenic height of land that drains south into Baker Creek and north into the Red Deer River. The bugs were not as bothersome here, so we rested, ate some GORP and checked out the area with binoculars. We saw two hikers across the valley on the lower slopes of Oyster Peak. We thought they might be wardens because they appeared to be wearing Parks

Canada shirts. We cruised slowly over the plateau, enjoying the sweeping views and the cooling breeze, then contoured down into a mature forest to reach the campground at Red Deer Lakes. It was just after noon and very warm, even in the plentiful shade. I set up the tent as Cecilia fixed some bannock for our noonday meal, and the bugs came to join us for lunch. They were not quite as bad here as they were at Baker Lake, but shortly after eating, we retired to the safety of the tent for a snooze.

This was one of the campgrounds which had a grizzly bear problem in July 1987 when a subadult female treed two hikers. After being chased off by a park warden from the Cyclone Cabin, the bruin moved on over to Merlin Meadows by the Skoki Lodge and frightened some campers there. On another day the bear wreaked havoc at Hidden Lake campground, the same night visiting an outfitters camp in the Little Pipestone Valley. In the space of five days, she had put 24 hikers up trees in five different locations. Wardens finally moved in and dispatched the aggressive bear. Parks personnel later speculated that the young bear was trying to establish herself in a new territory, and had chosen this rather bizarre way of doing it.

It was too hot to lie in the tent and worry about bears, and we were very anxious to explore this lovely area, so, with fleece and mosquito nets, gloves and toques, we walked out into the extensive meadows bathed in bright sunlight and temperatures of 28°C. We could wander at will there through dwarf willow that came up to our waists, enjoying views in every direction. I had been there once before, in 1970, and was so happy to be back.

In the fall of that year, I hiked through this region with two buddies, one of whom had spent the afternoon at the warden's cabin which he had located after some searching. I remembered that he had come back to our camp annoyed that we had not accompanied him on his quest. He had really wanted us to go, but we had wanted to go fishing, an activity for which he had little use. When asked about his afternoon, he remained taciturn and uncommunicative, "I'm not telling you what the warden had to say. If you want to know about the cabin, go find it yourself!" We, in turn, refused his request for sizzling, pan–fried trout, dripping in butter and onions.

Ever since, it seemed, I wanted to find that cabin, known as the Cyclone Warden Station, and so Cecilia and I made that our afternoon project. We followed a horse trail toward Hatchet Lake and soon saw an old corral fence, and in the distance, the warden patrol cabin. As we approached the small clearing in front of the cabin, a warden eased out through the screen door and hopped down off the porch. He was an easy–going fellow who gladly answered some questions we had about the area. He and his buddy had just come back from climbing Oyster Peak; it was them we had seen earlier in the day. We chatted for a while, then left and made our way to a rocky rib overlooking the Red Deer Lakes. As we left the pastureland by the cabin, his friendly horses came over, nudging us with their noses, looking for some oats.

What a sublime and peaceful area in which to have a cabin. Across the meadow, above the horses, Mounts Douglas and St. Bride caught the evening sun, the late winter snow still clinging to the higher ridges shimmered and danced with the intense light. Before our trip we had read that this particular cabin routinely files weather reports that chronicle some of the worst weather systems of any warden station in all four western national parks; maybe Cyclone Cabin is a fitting name!

We sat on the hillside into the early evening, watching the changing light as the sun dropped toward the distant summit of Mount Hector. It proved to be one of the most memorable evenings of the summer. The grasses on which we reclined were very similar to those found on the eastern slopes of the Rockies; the breeze was warm and kept the bugs away; the panorama before us continually changed with the setting sun. A string of horses crossed the meadow below us, their riders, from the outfitters camp some five kilometres down the valley, out for an evening on horseback. We wandered slowly back across the meadow, stopping several times to admire the twisting turns of the small brook that runs through it. Once in camp, we enjoyed a thorough washdown in the creek, then crawled into our tent to watch the light fade on Pipestone ridge.

~

As my sleeping spouse nestled in her warm cocoon I quietly left the tent as the morning sun crept into our meadow. After putting water on for coffee, I went out to photograph the sunrise on the distant peaks of Mount Hector and Molar Mountain. I paced back and forth through the willow shrubbery, looking for that special photo angle as the sun warmed my heart and soul. I felt wonderfully alive and alone out there on that summer morning. Sure there was another tent in our camp, yes Cecilia was nearby, but as I took in the incredible scenery, I felt so privileged to be there. There was an outfitters camp a few kilometres away and the wardens were over at the cabin, but still I felt the thrill of being alone. I casually imagined the distant city of Red Deer, a city out on the prairies 100 kilometres to the east. The early sun would be touching the buildings there, the people, still in the soft shadows of a new day commuting to work across the bridges that span the river. I wondered how many of Red Deer's residents knew the origin of their river. Had any of them ever seen the Red Deer Lakes; did any of them care? This morning I was the only one on Earth watching the sun sparkle on the brilliant waters of these lakes, and I felt honoured to be there.

Back in camp, I prepared coffee and retrieved the foodsack from the bear–hang as Cecilia emerged sleepily from the tent, coffee cup in hand. While she made porridge, I packed up the tent and got our gear in order for the day's hike to Merlin Meadows, near Skoki Lodge. Before shouldering our loads, we went over to look more closely at the largest of the Red Deer Lakes. It was a truly gorgeous day and we sat on the shore for a half–hour feeling the cool breeze that was blowing onshore and keeping the bugs at bay. The clear lake was several shades of blue, from the deepest indigo to the palest shades of green. Across the lake, two eagles swooped and dived about their nest, while behind us the ground squirrels squeaked and chased each other around the meadow.

On our return to camp, we met the three wardens from Cyclone Cabin, astride their horses, out for a patrol to Merlin Lake. They stopped and chatted a bit and looked so content in their saddles, so at home in their mountains, I was assailed with that old sting of jealousy. "Why, that should have been me." I had always wanted to be a park warden; had always wanted to roam these valleys.

We returned to our tent site, struggled into our backpacks and struck off for Jones Pass. The trail ascended moderately. We were on our own and, toward noon, we found ourselves on the pass sitting amongst the wildflowers, filtering four litres of water. We were always on the lookout for fresh, cool water, and reckoned that up here on the pass, the water would probably be safer to drink than the stream water that flowed past the lodge.

We then worked our way down from the pass and arrived at Skoki lodge in mid–afternoon.

~

Skoki Lodge is chock–full of history, dating back to the early '30s when Banff pioneers Cliff White and Cyril Paris skied through the area and thought it would be a great place for a ski lodge. The original log cabin was constructed in the Fall of 1931.

Ken Jones, a jack of all trades, helped them with their venture over the ensuing years. In 1936, they expanded the lodge, which required a new ridgepole some 60 feet in length. Jones, an expert axeman and woodsman eventually found a suitable tree 13 kilometres from the lodge. He returned to the area, near Douglas Lake, with a team of horses, dropped and trimmed the tree and, over a week, skidded it back to the lodge. In so doing, he discovered a short-cut, which later became known as Jones Pass.

Skoki Lodge sits near the tree line, at 2160 metres and has the distinction of being the highest backcountry lodge in any National Park in Canada. It accommodates 22 guests plus staff. The name "Skokie" which means "marshy," was suggested by John Porter, an American resident and the person credited with being the first to explore the many scenic attractions of the Skoki area. He was guided through this area in the summer of 1911.

We poked around inside the lodge for a bit, and left a message for my South African friends. Then, with lowering clouds and spitting rain, we wound our way down to the campground at Merlin Meadows, about a kilometre away. During the afternoon several hikers moved into camp. We were surprised by the number, as we had seen so few backpackers in the last couple of days.

We dined with the bugs that evening. We cooked up some pasta, while the bugs enjoyed their liquid meal, then later on, we went back to the lodge to visit with our friends. We were delighted to see each other again and, after I introduced Cecilia, we repaired to their cabin, the Wolverine, for refreshments and conversation.

The Wolverine Cabin has its own history. Originally it was a meat–storage facility. A wolverine broke into the cabin during a blizzard in 1936 and ate some of the meat, then left his stink over virtually everything inside. This is normal protocol for such an animal, his way of leaving sign, in this case through musky scent glands, to discourage other creatures from encroaching on his territory. This, of course, did nothing to endear him to the hearts of the lodge owners. He was subsequently caught while raiding the cabin again, and almost destroyed the place in his desperate and frenzied bid to escape. It was Ken Jones who eventually trapped the animal, using a coyote trap wired to a 4–foot log. Park warden Ulysses LaCasse shot the animal while it was still in the cabin. After it had been removed, the cabin logs were washed down with disinfectant to rid the area of smell.

Neil pulled out a bottle of scotch as well as some lemonade. There was lots of room in the old log structure, and it was a treat. I had thought we would visit in the lodge, or cram ourselves into a tiny bedroom upstairs; Wolverine was nothing short of palatial. Judith lit a kerosene lamp as the day faded and its warm, cheery glow on the historic and weathered logs made for a most relaxing evening. All too soon, the light faded from the sky and as we wanted to get back to our tent before it was fully dark, we bid our farewells.

~

The next morning was dreary, with pale sunlight on Mount Richardson. Swirling clouds and fog in the valley foretold a change in the weather. Our route that day lay west across the valley bottom and then up to Castilleja and Merlin Lakes. While coffee brewed, I visited with the bugs; they always seemed so happy to see me. Cecilia arose a little later and I let her value their incessant whining for a bit while I went down to the creek to wash out the coffee pot.

The trail from camp was, by turns, rutted, muddy, nonexistent, then boggy, before it climbed sharply over a rocky ridge to Castilleja Lake. The botanical name for Indian paintbrush, this aqua tarn is set into the forest in a small cirque–like impression. The grey morning accentuated its turquoise colour. We skirted the southeast shore and then climbed abruptly to another buttress adjoining a limestone bench just below Merlin Lake.

The famed coal–miner–turned–trail–builder, Lawrence Grassi undertook extensive rock work in this area to facilitate a gentler trail tread. His work seemed to border on the supernatural. A park warden once came across Grassi, who was busy restructuring a rough stone trail at Lake O'Hara. With a pry bar, he was wrestling with a slab of rock that must have weighed 400 pounds. The warden commented on how hard it must be to move such a gigantic boulder into position. Grassi looked up and wiped the sweat from his forehead. "All rocks will move," he said. "You just have to find the angle. If you can move it an inch, you can move it to Calgary!"

We climbed up over the rocky rib and into the cirque that held the lake. On a prettier day this area would be spectacular with the colour of the lake and the backdrop of the Richardson Glacier and snowfield. In 1928, the naturalist Charles Walcott wrote, "At the foot of the cliffs is a small sapphire–blue lake, fringed in July with Caltha (marsh marigold) and luxuriant emerald green sod." Today however, the lake's colour was decidedly monochromatic, and with a spitting rain and stiff breeze off the nearby icefield, the environs were less than stellar. Still, we were happy to have arrived at last. It was another one of those places I had always hoped to visit and I had now done so. The flower displays were magnificent; the showy paintbrush, fleabane and arnica nodded their heads in the fragrant breeze and begged for attention. At the end of the lake a scree slope rises to a rocky skyline col. From the top, this ridge offers views into the distant Bow Valley and farther west toward Mounts Cathedral and Stephen, peaks that rise above the town of Field, in British Columbia.

We took a different path back down, a horse trail not often used by hikers. At the bottom, we crossed Skoki Creek without the benefit of a bridge, but we had expected that considering it was a horse trail. We continued to the lodge on an older pathway that follows the creek drainage. It is a fine trail and offers views of the canyon worn into the bedrock by the stream. I had no idea there was a canyon around here. We arrived at the lodge in mid–afternoon and listened to the far–off rumblings of thunder. It was becoming hostile outside, and we agreed that tea and sweet cakes in the warmth of the lodge would be a swell way to pass the afternoon. As the rain descended, I held to my belief that every raindrop kills a bug.

We stayed in the sanctuary of the lodge for a couple of hours visiting with various guests. Cecilia and I laid plans for a future trip to this historic treasure. The lodge's wood fire ambiance in the Fall, when the golden larches are on parade would be a tonic for the soul. There are so many places to explore here, and the country would be a riot of colour in the frosty autumn season.

We walked down to our wet tent in showery weather, made dinner and then dropped into the tent for a relaxing evening of reading. The sombre twilight and the soothing pattern of the rain on the tent fabric induced a restful slumber.

~

Hoping to catch the sunrise on Mount Richardson, I was out of the tent at first light but was thwarted in my endeavours. High cloud–cover diffused the light as the weak sun filtered through the forest. We packed up and left for our next camp at Hidden Lake. En route we chatted with two hikers who had started at Mount Norquay ski area and hiked into Flints Park, over Badger Pass, then down to the Baker Creek drainage, over Jones Pass and on to Skoki. They said they had travelled for four days without seeing a soul. I was always amazed at the ambitious plans of some of the trekkers I met.

Our route was over Packer's Pass. At 2475 metres, this is the highest pass I would traverse that season. Over the summer, I would hike over 17 passes with varying elevations. A high elevation does not necessarily indicate a hard passage, and a pass at a lower elevation also does not always mean that it is easy to negotiate. Passes are like doors; when the pass is crested, or the door is opened, one can see what lies beyond. The last few plodding steps before reaching the pass reveal little other than frost shattered rock directly in front of your eyes. Then, suddenly, you are atop the pass and can see into the next valley, sometimes for miles, and you gaze with fascination and delight at sights denied just moments before.

We crossed the open forest below the Skoki Lakes and ascended an artfully–contrived rock staircase cleverly built into a chimney system below the first lake. These lakes were also given names by the Porter party when they visited here in 1911. Commonly referred to today as the Skoki Lakes, they are in fact, Myosotis (forget–me–not) Lake and Zigadenus (Camas lily) Lake. The day was dull, and we hiked around to our left and climbed up a steep headwall to the second lake which lay tucked under Ptarmigan Peak. Here we relaxed for an hour, eating, taking in the sights and enjoying each other's company. An old Hollies song came to mind… "all I need is the air that I breathe and to love you."

In worsening conditions, we struck out for the pass, and with perfect timing, crested out just as a sleet storm blew in. Icy pellets stung our faces in the driving wind, but the storm was short lived thankfully and quickly moved on down the valley to hopefully slaughter those damn bugs at Baker Lake.

We descended from these bleak environs, staying high as we traversed to Boulder Pass. Arriving at Hidden Lake campground later in the afternoon we set up our tent to the accompaniment of ominous thunder rolling across the peaks. Dinner was early, as we expected rain at any moment, however, it held off.

Two climbers, Mike and Terry, were in the tent next to us and they came over for a visit. They had scrambled up Fossil Mountain that day and hoped to do a traverse of Richardson, Pika and Ptarmigan mountains on the next day, weather permitting. We looked southwest to the Valley of the Ten Peaks on the Continental Divide. Purple thunderheads were gathering; lightning played amongst their lofty summits and the air seemed full of evil portent. It was much darker than normal for this time of evening and as we watched, fat raindrops began falling in our little valley. We all ducked into our tents just as the skies opened up and a strong rain hammered the campsite. Near dark, the rain ended and as the air seemed so fresh and clean it seemed possible the next day would be fine.

Blue sky and a rich morning sun greeted us, and we scurried from the tent for the final day of the hike. We decided to forego breakfast. Our imagination had convinced us that we could smell bacon, eggs and coffee wafting up the valley from distant Lake Louise! As I packed the tent away, Mike and Terry were dancing a jig; they were so excited that they would have a good day for their traverse, given the weather conditions of the previous evening.

Pink and orange clouds drifted lazily over the summit of Mount Richardson as we strapped our packs on and headed down to the trail past Halfway Hut. Hiking through the mountains that early morning, with tendrils of mist lying over Corral Creek, was emotionally and visually stimulating. We were the first up and on the trail and we walked in the dark, cool shade from Redoubt Mountain while across the valley, the sun warmed the grassy slopes of the Lake Louise ski area. This early time of day was a magical and mystical time for me: the exhilarating, tangy freshness of the dawn, the way the sunlight warms the mountains.

The newness of the day was intoxicating. I always seem to get so much out of these mountain mornings. I skipped down the trail with wings on my boots.

As we were hiking along, (thankfully I had finished skipping) we met some fishermen coming up the trail to try their luck in Redoubt Lake. We knew they would do well. When we hiked there in 1997 the anglers on the lake were having a great day. We had watched with envy as almost every cast produced a brook trout or a cutthroat. We wished the fishermen good luck and continued on. Farther down we surprised two deer as they crossed our trail and before long, we were back at our truck. It had taken us less than two hours to descend from Hidden Lake.

~

We sat down to a table at a coffee shop in Lake Louise, and as we sipped our coffee and looked around, we felt like a pair of aliens. It was a shock from what we had been used to. Here we could eat our food at leisure (there were no bugs to frustrate us), the bacon smelled great, we had not had toast for some time, we had a real table with cutlery and table napkins, and even a padded chair to sit on.

After our meal, Cecilia went shopping for steaks and French bread for our supper while I went to the outdoor store in search of some boot insoles. On this trip, my heels had become increasingly painful and I thought perhaps it could be from a lack of a proper footbed. Earlier in the year, I had bought some orthotics for my new boots: form–fitted insoles whose purpose was to realign my foot and ankle skeletal structure to better facilitate load carrying. I should have known better. My feet and ankles could not and should not be realigned after 54 years, so I had discarded them. I was then without insoles of any type, and my heels were beginning to feel the pack weight. At Lake Louise I was able to get just what I required, a foam insole with an extra cushion under the heel. It was an immediate relief, and I used them for the rest of the summer with fantastic results.

From Lake Louise we went to the Johnston Canyon campground for some rest and relaxation. This was a transition day, the time between finishing one hike and preparing for the next one. We checked into the campsite, then grabbed our towels and some soap and made a beeline to the shower house. After a long, long hot shower, we felt we could once again fit in with the general populace. Over by the truck, we spent the afternoon drinking rum with real ice, playing cards, and reminiscing about our hike into Skoki. We lounged and snoozed in our comfy camp chairs. Then I fired up the barby and the steaks sizzled in the warm evening air. We ate lots of fresh fruit, and still had some room for Black Forest cake!

That evening, in the late twilight, we meandered over to the Bow River and watched the evening shadows play on the peaks of Castle, Copper and Pilot mountains. Late that night, as we lay in the truck on eight inches of luxurious foam, our sleepy smiles reflected our contentment with the past week.

The verses in this chapter are from the poem The Legend of Halfway Hut by John Porter published in *Timberline Tales*, Jim Deegan & John Porter, The Peter Whyte Foundation: Banff, 1977. © Mrs. Helen Porter. All rights reserved.

Rainy Days on the Rockwall

The Rockwall Trail proved to be one of the most arduous hikes of the summer. The 55–kilometre trail is demanding and includes four high passes. The total elevation gain is somewhere around 2500 metres, with steep descents covering about 2300 metres. I had set aside five days for this hike, believing it to be the most scenically rewarding route in Kootenay National Park.

On the morning of July 15, I sat at the table in the Johnston Canyon campground and wolfed down bacon, eggs and hash browns, fresh bread, kiwi fruit and raspberries. Hot coffee filtered into the last recesses of my stomach, and I sat back, for the moment, satiated. I had enjoyed a deep rest in the back of the truck and was now ready for my appointment with the Rockwall.

We decamped early in the morning and Cecilia swung the truck over towards Kootenay National Park. I munched on an apple as she threaded her way through the heavy, summer tourist traffic, and I was reminded yet again that it was far more dangerous out there on the highway than in the deepest, darkest corner of any National Park. We arrived at the Floe Lake trailhead, hugged each other desperately, and I was off on another adventure.

The trail was like an old friend; I had visited this area three or four times over the years and eagerly anticipated the alpine beauty of Floe Lake. I had about 11 kilometres to hike and all day to do it. I set an easy pace, as I knew the headwall just below the lake is brutal; with the pack on, it would be an endurance test. The day was not overly warm—some high cirrus hid the sun—but it was uncommonly muggy. There was some hiker traffic on the trail, which was fine with me, as several avalanche slopes crossed the route. With the prolific vegetative growth, including devils club and cow parsnip covering the slopes, sight lines were reduced; it would be hard to spot any furry denizens that were known to inhabit these open areas.

Soon the headwall came into view and the trail charged up into the forest. In less than three kilometres, it climbed 400 metres into the sub–alpine environs of Floe Lake. I felt that I was prepared, as I had "been there, done that" on other occasions over the years. I drained a litre of water and was sure that I would pound right up this trail without even stopping. It turned out to be a lot more demanding than I remembered, however, and I was huffing and grunting almost immediately. In no time sweat was pouring down my face and into my eyes. I started looking for the telltale larches that would signal that the height–gain was almost over. But the path continued it's brutal attack, and the hoped for larches were an apparent figment of my imagination. I climbed up and up, seemingly forever, and I began to wonder if I was going to make it before dark!

It then became even steeper and I fantasized that perhaps I should be roping up, maybe even placing a piton or two for protection! This precipitous rise to the alpine, the sheer diabolical nature of the trail, was bringing out the sarcasm in me. Just where the heck is tree line around here anyway, 14,000 feet maybe? I had no water left and I kicked myself for not having brought more along. I was starting to feel very dehydrated, delirious and disenchanted with the whole deal and so I stopped, rested, and ate a power bar. I tried to regain my perspective. I looked over my shoulder up through the trees to the grey sky, in a forlorn search for the larches; where were they? I pushed myself to my feet and, somewhat energized by the rest and energy bar, continued on. I dared not look farther up the headwall; it was just too demoralizing. Instead, I concentrated on watching my dusty boots, and a few minutes later saw some old, tan larch needles embedded in the trail tread and knew the worst was over. A few more steps and I caught my first glimpse of the slate–grey waters of Floe Lake.

My pack crashed to the ground like a sack full of anvils and I toured through the campground, looking about for a suitable site. There were only two tents pitched so far, and I took the last site that had a lake view. It had taken me four and a half–hours to get in there, the guidebook had said four, and so I felt a small measure of relief. Still, I had a long summer ahead of me if all the ascents were going to intimidate me as this one just had.

I remembered a stream that flowed past the warden cabin a few hundred metres from the campground and hustled over to get some water to filter. The clouds were lowering and a light sprinkle of rain descended on the camp. I wrapped my food in some plastic and suspended it from the bear–hang, then pitched the tent and threw the pack inside before anything could become damp. I too climbed into the tent and rested, out of the weather for an hour or so.

Over the next few hours, several hikers came into camp and by nightfall there must have been at least a dozen tents dispersed throughout the larches. The evening was very grey and windless and so, after dinner, I wandered down to the end of the lake, the flowers along the lakeshore the only companions I needed. I sat near the end of the lake for an hour, my back against a rock and watched the subtle breezes play over the water. It was sombre and quiet down there at that end and the funereal sky made the Rockwall slabs above the lake virtually featureless, but for the ring of snow along the base that feeds into the icy water.

I returned to camp with some more water to treat and sat by the tent. Up until this year, I had never bothered to treat the water I collected in the mountains and I was not convinced I needed to now. Parks information pamphlets urging hikers to do so had put a scare into me. The main reason for treating all surface water before drinking was to avoid contracting the parasite, *Giardia lamblia*. It gets into the water when a carrier defecates near or in a water source. Being well informed is part of being a responsible backpacker and it does make sense to err on the side of caution. And so, I now do filter my water.

Over at the next tent site, I had a chinwag with Ken and Wanda, two friendly folks from Vancouver. They ran an outdoor adventure concern on the West Coast and were presently on a fact–gathering holiday. The three of us spent some time exchanging wilderness philosophies and gazing out over the lake. Most everyone else was back in the trees, away from the scenery and we congratulated ourselves on securing two of the best sites around. Sometimes it pays to hit the trail early!

I woke up very early the next day in order to catch the morning light on the vertical limestone face above the lake. I wandered through the tents quietly. With 30 some hikers here, I was the only one up and about. This was to be a long day for me, almost 18 kilometres with two passes to negotiate, and so I put together a large breakfast and drained a litre of water. The sky was a deep, indigo blue that morning and it induced me to get going, as I wanted to arrive at Numa Pass in good weather for what would assuredly be some dynamite photos! I hustled to get my pack together and was able to get underway quickly. As I left the camp, one sleepy hiker was making her way down to the lake.

I climbed up through the open forest above Floe Lake and the feathery larches were lime green in the early morning sun. A hundred metres above the lake, I turned to take a picture and was quite surprised to see a wall of grey cloud scudding in from the west; apparently this day was not going to be quite as sunny and camera–friendly as I had presumed.

As I traversed the alpine tundra near Numa Pass, a couple of hikers caught up and passed me as I took some parting pictures of Floe Lake far below. The lake was named for small icebergs that occasionally calve into the lake. Snow builds up on the northeast face of the sheer cliffs above the lake, deposited there by the prevailing winds, forming what are sometimes referred to as drift glaciers. Every once in a while large chunks of ice break away and fall into the lake.

Numa is a word from the Cree language and means thunder. It was getting ready to do precisely that as I stood on top of the pass. It was decidedly chilly and windy up there above the trees, and I quickly moved off to the north side of the pass and into the lee of the prevailing breeze. I rested and ate some crackers and cheese and gazed across the intervening valleys to the distant peaks that rise above Lake Louise.

The trail down to Numa Creek was described in my trail guide as one of the most abrupt in the National Parks, descending over 800 metres in a mere seven kilometres. I took it easy and was overtaken by a dozen or more hikers whose knees were apparently much younger than mine. Deep down in the forest, a log spanned the south fork of Numa Creek. At this point the creek was four metres wide, almost a metre deep, and moving very swiftly as it churned its way down to the Vermilion River. There were a few hikers standing about when I arrived. They all seemed rather reluctant to cross as the felled log was about two metres above the raging water. It was only 14 inches wide, and bounced in an alarming fashion as each person crossed.

Later on in the summer, after the worst of the runoff, most hikers would probably just rock–hop this particular ford, but that was not an option for us on this day. I loosened both my pack straps and hip belt as my turn came and proceeded across; if the unthinkable happened and I lost my balance, I wanted to be able to quickly jettison the pack in the stream to save myself from getting hung up in a log jam.

Thoughts of a log crossing on the way to Connor Lakes long ago flashed through my mind. I had slipped right off that log and been dragged under by the turbulent stream. Fortunately, the water's velocity had flushed me through to a downstream pool. Numa Creek had a lot more volume and the log spanning it was much higher. With a 50–pound pack, an accident could prove to be very serious and it was good to have other hikers about, just in case. We all stayed to make sure none of us took a bath, then moved on down the trail to the Numa Creek campground for lunch.

There were about ten of us there, gathering strength for the next part of the trail, which was the gruelling 750–metre ascent to the glades of Tumbling Pass. It was here, in this campground, where I first heard that a "curious" grizzly had been roaming through the vicinity. A warden back on the highway had advised some hikers not to stay here at Numa Campground, as they had planned, but instead move on to Tumbling Pass Campground, another eight kilometres along the trail. This camping spot was not in my plans anyway, and I headed out to tackle the steep trail to the pass.

I had been over this trail many years before and had thought it fairly straightforward. What I had not remembered was the closed–in feeling caused by the lush vegetation on the avalanche slopes. Here the cow parsnip grew above my head and obscured my vision and the roaring stream coming down from the pass made it impossible to hear anything. I knew that I should be making some noise here—this looked like prime grizzly habitat—and I recalled that the author of my trail guide had referred to this part of the

Rockwall Trail as "a grizzly grocery store." I reflected again on the warden's selected adjective, "curious." I guess it could have been worse, he could have used "aggressive" or "threatening." As I pondered his choice of adjectives I saw the first bear scat. I could not be sure how recent it was, but its presence put me on "red alert." I blew my whistle and hollered out what I hoped was a friendly salutation, "yo bear!" I knew my voice would carry only a few feet over the sound of the cascading melt water foaming along beside the trail. Then I saw the next bear scat, and a little farther on, a very large and much fresher–looking dump spread across the trail in an untidy mess. It was here that I decided to call a halt. My eyes were darting from bush to stream, from boulder to hillside. I knew the bruin might be miles away but I was also aware of my vulnerability, travelling on my own. I knew that there were two hikers perhaps 30 minutes ahead of me on the trail and two more not far behind, so I sat down to wait for the latter, Steve and Marilyn. We had helped each other out earlier in the day, crossing the log on Numa Creek and they would now be of help to me. They were from Oakland, California and I wasn't sure how they would interpret the bear sign. Would they even know it was bear dung? Hell, even I didn't know if it was black bear or grizzly poop!

Steve rounded the corner first, and his posture looked defensive, as if he was in a back alley in New York at midnight. He saw me up ahead and his face lit up in a happy grin and with typical American bravado hollered, "Man, hey dude, talk about in your face bear shit! You been checking this out?" I most certainly had, and suggested perhaps we should travel through this ursine salad feast together. He had an even better idea, "Why don't we just rest here for a bit, shoot the breeze and filter some water, because I know there's another couple coming up behind us. Maybe they should join in and then all our problems will be over!"

Five minutes later, Nancy and Lutz showed up. They were glad to see reinforcements. As it turned out they were the ones who had been cautioned by the park warden who they had met at Marble Canyon two days previously. The warden who had used the word "curious." This "scientific catchphrase" apparently meant that while this particular young grizzly had not yet threatened any hikers, he had been amusing himself by standing up on his hind legs just to watch the passing hikers freak out. He was a bear simply full of pure adolescent devilry! Nancy and Lutz were told to be watchful and definitely not camp overnight at Numa.

And so it was that the five of us climbed the remaining two kilometres to the sub–alpine meadows of Tumbling Pass. Once up in the alpine and away from the perceived threat, we split up, agreeing to have dinner together that evening at camp. I was quickly left to the rear as I stopped to watch three goats on a rock shelf close to the trail. The meadows about were strewn with wildflowers and captured my attention as I passed. The clouds were streaming in over the limestone cliffs, and it looked like it might become a damp evening. It was getting close to dinnertime and I still had three kilometres to go. I took some photos of the anemone and paintbrush that carpet the alpine fields here, then hurried on across the high bench land toward camp. To the north I saw the Wolverine Plateau partly obscured by the wind–torn clouds. Three hundred and thirty metres below I could see bright splashes of colour in the meadow; the tents a vivid contrast to the darkness of the surrounding forest.

The wind picked up and a distant rumbling filled the valley. I wished that I was already down off this exposed ridge, safe in my tent. I galloped along as fast as possible, but just as I crossed the bridge below camp, the rain caught me. Mere yards from camp, I was forced to stop, take off the pack and search out my rain gear. The campground was laid out well. Gravelled paths led to flat tent sites, and the food area replete with new cooking tables, was scenically located near the creek. In the driving rain, however, it was difficult to appreciate. Everyone here, it seemed, was out of the weather, safe in his or her tent while I fumbled around looking for a site. I hastily shook out the tent and got it set up and pegged down, then jumped inside to wait out the shower. In an hour the rain had passed down the valley and the air became crisp and cool. I boiled my water for dinner and wolfed down my soup and crackers as another storm approached.

After washing up the dishes in the nearby stream, I trundled over to use the facilities and found the outhouse to be virtually in ruins! In the damp twilight I moved on over to the other outhouse down at the far end of the campground. I pried open the door on squeaking, rusty hinges. Squinting into the murky beyond however, I saw that this particular seat was taken. By a porcupine! He was actually perched right on the toilet seat and peered at me with little porcine eyes and his head weaving and ducking from side to side as he tried to focus on me. Mumbling an insincere apology, I moved away and off into the woods. I came back into camp and realized I had had quite enough of my day and so, as it promised to be a wet and miserable night, and as all the other hikers were ensconced in their colourful cocoons, I tucked in to my bag to read as the silt–laden Tumbling Creek rumbled away in the gathering gloom.

~

While I was camped in perhaps the prettiest campground of the entire summer, the morning of July 17 was undoubtedly the most dismal. I woke several times during the night to the sound of a heavy rain pelting the tent. I lay in my warm, dry bag as the weak, suffused light of dawn came into the tent and pensively considered my options. Usually when backpacking, there are few alternatives, but here, in this particular campground, there did exist a couple of choices. I could either just sit it out and be tentbound for the day or get up and get going. The other possibility, of course, was to quit, leave the hike here by descending Tumbling Creek, to the highway, about 11 kilometres away. I discarded that bleak option right away; after all, it was only wet weather!

With the incessant rain tapping on my tent, I put on my rain gear and hunched out through the fly into the cold and dreary dawn. It was worse than I thought. The rain–saturated cloud ceiling was very low, perhaps 70 metres above the tent. The Wolverine Plateau was about 370 metres above the campground and shrouded in 300 metres of fog and rain. There were 10 or 12 tents scattered about but all was silent, except for the dripping rain. Nobody was up and I couldn't blame them. I rustled up some coffee and porridge under the protective branches of a fir tree and for a brief second became encouraged as the swirling mass of cloud lifted, only to reveal the disheartening spectre of fresh snow on the talus fans.

The rain eased off, and it was sure funny to watch the tents suddenly come alive; they started shaking and trembling as people moved about inside, no doubt cheered by the fact that the rain had stopped. I sat under a tree on a comfortable bed of needles, sipping my rum–laced brew and gazed ruefully up at the fresh snow. My fellow hikers were in for a rude surprise when they crawled out to greet the morning!

As I moved through the cooking area, everyone there preparing their meals seemed to have varying opinions. Two tents were already packing up and bailing out. Another tent was going to stay here for the day. Nancy and Lutz were going to pack up, drink a pail of coffee, and "wait and see." In the tent next to mine, Neil and Michelle decided they were going to continue on, snow wasn't going to bother them! If the rain kept up, they would continue on down to Ochre Creek, 21 kilometres away. I made the decision to continue, hoping the weather would improve. I didn't want to quit; I had a great summer planned, and a little rain never hurt. Or snow, for that matter.

Things were starting to get very wet—my boots and socks were pretty soaked, but my sleeping bag was still dry, and the tent was holding up very well. My pack was wet, but so far the stuff inside the pack was just clammy, damp and cold. I shouldered it and moved out across the meadow, planning to stop by Marilyn and Steve's tent to see if they would be continuing. I had figured them to be a tough pair and so I was surprised when I saw them coming toward me in the misty rain. Steve still wore his cheerful grin, but his face looked awfully red. Marilyn explained that their stove had blown up in Steve's face; his eyebrows were gone, and his eyelashes seem glued together, but he was okay. They had lost all their fuel in the accident and because they had no way to heat their meals, they were forced to exit the Rockwall Trail at this point. We said our goodbyes and I went up along the trail by myself. Before long, Neil and Michelle caught up and passed me. Their day was going to be over 20 kilometres, so in view of the inclement weather, they were setting a fast pace for themselves.

As I approached the alpine environment of the Wolverine plateau, the drizzle slackened off and a strong westerly wind started to rip the clouds apart. Still clinging to the wet tundra grasses, the snow of the previous night was fast disappearing and a weak, cool sun peeped between the storm clouds. I had hoped to go over and visit the warden cabin located in this alpine field and then take the short side trip to Wolverine Pass. I propped my pack up against a rock outcrop and skirted a grassy hummock to look over the plateau. In the distance, perhaps 300 metres away, the rustic old cabin sat in a grove of young larch. The trail here was vague and the soaking grasses seemed to be turning my boots to mush! The cabin was not appealing to the photographer in me, and so I turned and headed over to Wolverine Pass.

The actual height of land lay between Mount Gray and Mount Drysdale. It was a windy, narrow defile and offered lonesome views west down the Dainard Creek drainage to the Beaverfoot Valley. I stood on the boundary of Kootenay National Park. Apparently there is a logging road down below in the trees that comes to within two kilometres of the pass. Hence, the strategically placed warden cabin, which is there to protect the resident wildlife from the poaching lowlife. The mountains on either side of the pass, mounts Gray and Drysdale, were named in remembrance of two gentlemen from the Provincial Boundary Commission who drowned in the Kootenay River in 1917 when they were in the area doing geological field work.

Back on the main trail once again, I traversed the barren meadows toward Rockwall Pass, which sits at an elevation of 2250 metres. The windy day bestowed upon this bleak area a certain austerity and I felt quite apart from the civilized world up there. I knew there would probably be hikers coming along the trail behind me, but for the time being, this place was all mine. The air was refreshing after the heat of the previous weeks and I was amazed at how energetic I felt. It is here, on the pass, that the Rockwall's scenery is at its finest. The walls rise almost straight up, in some places 300 metres above the trail. This wall of limestone stretches over 50 kilometres in a north–westerly direction and forms the boundary of Kootenay National Park. In all my travels, I can think of nothing that compares to this imposing mountain wall.

From this high point, the trail winds its way down into the larches to a bridge across the south fork of Helmet Creek It was here that I encountered two other hikers coming up toward me, the only ones I would see all day. It had started raining again so our trailside chitchat was brief. We moved apart in the rain toward our respective destinations.

The trail up to Limestone summit was lush and green and lined with many uniquely shaped larches. Near the top, at 2190 metres, the rain turned into a sleet–snow mixture accompanied by a strong wind, and the view was obliterated by a passing tempest. The sound of remote Helmet Falls met my ears as I scampered down into the trees to avoid the sleet.

Helmet Falls, is arguably the fourth–highest falls in Canada, cascades from a cliff face almost 400 metres high. Its roar was a constant companion for the rest of the day. The 500–metre descent to the alluvial outwash at the base of the falls was fraught with slippery rocks and exposed roots and my walking poles proved very helpful as I negotiated the steep trail. Once down, I breathed a sigh of relief; falling with a 50 pound pack was never far from my mind.

However, as I crossed a boggy wetland on some greasy, rain–slicked logs, in the blink of an eye, down I went. One foot twisted off the log into calf–deep black sludge, while the other skidded out ahead without purchase; my pack torqued my lower back and I fell shoulder first onto the log. My bare forearm took most of the weight and I scraped along on the log for a while, affecting the pose of a skateboarder doing the rails in a park! I rolled off the log and into the mud, my pack doing a credible job of pile driving my head into the odorous muck. With 50 pounds on my neck, I rose unsteadily from the quagmire on hands and knees, feeling just like the "Creature from the Black Lagoon." I had come close to breaking my forearm. I was only a half kilometre from camp and though I was no wetter, I was certainly much dirtier. It was indeed lucky for me that it was raining so hard, as I would be pretty much rinsed off before entering the campground.

Neil and Michelle were there on my arrival; they had passed me earlier in the day on the approach to the Wolverine plateau. They decided to continue down to the Ochre Creek campground as the day was miserable and they thought that they might as well hike as sit in a wet tent. I elected to stay. I was hoping to photograph Helmet Falls if the weather improved that evening or early the next morning.

A wardens' cabin across the creek was occupied by a trail maintenance crew. It was too wet for them to work, and they looked pretty snug and warm over there with wood–smoke curling from the chimney pipe. I was kind of hoping that if I stood around long enough, looking like a drowned dog, they might pop out for an instant and offer me a mug of hot chocolate and a chance to dry out my socks, but of course it never happened.

I set up my soaking wet tent in continuous rain and sought refuge inside. The tent was amazingly dry, but everything I brought in was soggy and damp. My boots and socks were sodden, all my clothes were clammy and my stove was getting harder to light, as moisture seeped in around the orifices. I retired to my sleeping bag and read and wrote for a couple of hours while various hikers came dripping into camp, their boots squelching in the trailside mud. I could hear them as they passed, grumbling and muttering about the rain and in a hurry to set up their own tents. Over dinner that evening in the drizzle, I decided to finish this hike on the next day. The showery weather persisted as darkness filled the valley.

~

The night was full of steady rain and blustery weather. The strong wind would come down off the shoulder of Helmet, and sweep across the alluvial flats to slam into the forest where our tents were nestled. Often during that dark night, a blast of wind would hit my tent causing it to balloon out snapping taut against the fibreglass poles. Close to daylight, it became quite calm, but the rain intensified. The feeble light of a cold dawn filled my clammy abode and I got dressed in the dampness and went outside. There was fresh snow at tree line and a solid mass of rain–soaked cloud above. Even the sound of the falls seemed muted in this soggy solitude. I found a dry spot under a spruce tree near camp and prepared some coffee and porridge. It was indeed a bleak morning, no smoke rose from the cabin chimney on the opposite side of the creek, and everyone was hunkered down, snug in their tents. I drained the last of my coffee, rinsed the cup in the creek and prepared to leave.

Once on the trail, and away from the dreariness of the campground, I began to appreciate the day, the quiet solitude, the dripping green canopy above. The only sound was the plop, plop of the rain and the plod, plod of the hiker. The trail was inundated with runoff and the rain collected in pools that in some cases were two metres long and deeper than my boot tops, as I quickly discovered! I was not bothered because my boots could not possibly become wetter. The suspension bridge across the swollen Helmet Creek was an exciting challenge; the rain–slick deck was treacherous and swayed under my weight as I crossed the cabled structure.

Helmet Creek, in this constricted valley takes on a lot of character, with a host of rapids and foaming whitewater as it surges headlong down the valley in its rush to meet the distant Vermilion River. Other than the stream, nothing moved in this wet environment, no birds, no squirrels, no bugs, just the spreading leaves of the cow parsnip as the fat drops of rain fell upon them.

By mid–morning I had pulled in to the Ochre Creek campground. This was supposed to be my home for the night, but with the continuing rain, I decided to conclude my trip one day early. This decision posed a bit of a dilemma. Cecilia would not be at the trailhead for another day, and she of course had no way of knowing that I was coming out from the Rockwall earlier than planned. I wasn't going to sit on the highway for a day waiting for my ride and I didn't feel like hanging around at Ochre Creek all day, with no chance of building a fire and drying out. I sat by the creek and munched a power bar and pondered. I decided to hitch a ride over to the Columbia Valley where Cecilia and Cindy, my younger daughter, were visiting. As I hiked the remaining six kilometres to the Marble Canyon trailhead, I felt quite confident about securing passage with some highway voyager.

I rounded a corner on the trail and was unceremoniously debouched into a maelstrom of tourist traffic at the Marble Canyon Paint Pots. Every manner and shape of tourist was represented here, and I had to remind myself that at least they were showing some interest in the local history of this region by visiting the interpretive signs spaced throughout the Ochre beds. During the last century, the Kutenai Indians from the west had come here to the paint pots to collect the ochre–coloured mud. The clay, which was dyed red from leaching iron oxides, was used in trade with the Plains tribes. The Kutenais would dry the clay into cakes and transport them by horse up the valley I had just descended. They would go over Goodsir Pass and down the Ottertail River to its junction with the Kicking Horse River, a junction that is today just west of Field, B.C. From here they would ford the Kicking Horse River, and ascend the Amiskiwi River, to the pass of the same name. They then would travel up the Blaeberry River to Howse Pass, and down the Howse River to its confluence with the North Saskatchewan River. It was along this river, as they approached the Kootenay Plains, that they would meet other Aboriginal tribes from the prairies and conclude their trading. The valley I had just spent the morning descending was rich with history, a prominent trade route for native tribes. It had been an enriching experience to travel in their footsteps.

I reached the highway about midday. The pavement was wet, though not nearly as soaked as I, and as the motor homes hissed by on their way to sunnier climes the rain came pelting down. I started humming an old Doors tune, "Riders on the Storm." I sure hoped nobody around here knew the words to that particular ditty, or I would never get a ride! My dishevelled appearance was, I realized, somewhat disquieting to these highway travellers and the diesel choked turbulence of their rapid passing threatened to roll me off the highway shoulder. I was muddy and wet and in need of a shave and a bath. In addition, I was the owner of a soaking wet 50–pound pack. Now who, do you suppose, would pick up an anomaly such as this in the middle of who knows where? Why hippies from California, that's who! They had a rusted–out VW bus. A young wisp of a girl was at the helm, her lank blond hair doing its best to hide the road from her eyes. One look at her transported me back 35 years, but I jumped in anyway, just happy to be out of the rain. Her hippy buddy in the back had an afro, and was reclining in some sort of fake vinyl, duct–taped Lazy–Boy. Now I knew where the name came from, I thought. He was replete with beads and beard and that vacant look that all parents hate. His eyes peered at me through little round dark blue glasses and he nodded, "Hey dude."

The pungent smell of recently smoked ganga hung in the air, and I saw what looked like a hookah pipe on the floor. If I kept looking about, I just knew I would find an old eight–track tape featuring Jimi Hendrix! The driver told me she attended college in Sacramento, while the spaced out visage behind was a self–styled fire eater. They were in the process of gradually winding their way back home. Yes, it was 1960 again. These strangers were polite and very cool and I yearned to go back to that gentler era. I bummed a ride with them for 20 minutes to Vermilion Crossing. It was raining buckets, yet the driver did not feel the need to turn on her windshield wipers. There was no wiper on my side anyway, just a twisted, rusted metal arm.

At Vermilion Crossing, I tried to phone Cecilia in the valley, but there was unfortunately, no phone service at the crossing. It was probably all for the best, I'd forgotten how to use a phone anyway. I reflected on my new lifestyle, tramping through the bush, getting healthier by the hour, and getting sun burned teeth from grinning so much. I had no current job and I was starting to hang with the hippies. Man I was having fun! But I needed another ride over to the Columbia Valley.

I went into the washroom and amazingly enough found some hot water! No phone, but damn, we got the hot water! I donned some fairly clean, dry clothes though I could do nothing about my boots. They seemed destined to stay wet for years to come. Back in the parking lot, I immediately secured a ride. These tourists even had room for my gigantic, dripping pack in their little rental Toyota Tercel. They were visiting from Germany and though they were a little disappointed with the weather, they were happy to give me a lift and learn some of the local history. It rained steadily all the way to Radium.

That afternoon, I sat in Cindy's house with Cecilia, swapping stories and drinking wine. My gear, including the pack and tent, was outside drying on the wash line and my clothes were washed and tumbling in the warm dryer. I kept looking up at the ceiling, as I hadn't seen one for a few weeks. It seemed incredible that just six hours ago, I had been climbing out of a dripping tent at Helmet Falls. That evening we cooked some steaks on the barby, and I had a dry place to sleep; yes, all was fine again. The next day my taxi driver, Cecilia, would chauffeur me back to the Bow Valley where I would set out on my next excursion.

To Marvel pass

Alex and I stood in the Sunshine parking lot at the base of the tram, on the hot summer morning of July 20, preparing our packs for our hike through Mount Assiniboine Provincial Park.

He was a friend of mine from back home. At a party a few months earlier, he had been most interested in my hiking plans for the summer. I suggested that he should come along on one or two of them and he immediately jumped at the opportunity to hike with me into Mount Assiniboine.

We were engrossed in our first problem of the day; he wanted to hike the six kilometres up to the Sunshine Village ski area, while I campaigned for the bus. The memory of trudging up the Temple Lodge access road two weeks earlier was still fresh in my mind, although I did feel a little guilty starting a wilderness outing on a bus. Alex wanted the experience to be unsullied by motorized transport, so he elected to walk. He allowed himself however, a small measure of guilt by having the bus take his backpack up the road for him!

As the old school bus churned up the dusty road, I thought of what lay ahead for us. This trip would take us eight days, and we would travel through about 70 kilometres of sub–alpine beauty. For most of the route, we would be rubbing shoulders with the Continental Divide, camping in the larches, and hiking over Citadel, Wonder and Marvel passes. It was hard to believe we were going to see more than twenty backcountry lakes and tarns!

The morning air was fresh and clear at the ski hill, and I waited for Alex to make his way up, which he did a mere five minutes later, riding in the back of a dusty blue Chevy work truck. His guilt apparently, didn't extend to procuring a free ride in someone else's maintenance vehicle! His cheeky grin spoke volumes; "Ha, so here we both are, but you *paid* for *your* ride"!

We lost little time in escaping the cumulative clutter about the ski resort. I've noticed this before at other ski hills. An alpine resort can look so pristine and picture–postcard beautiful in winter with a thick mantle of snow, but summertime produces a different image. With no snow to hide its imperfections, the area appears unkempt. It's times like this when one queries why something of this intrusive nature would ever be allowed in a National Park. Wildflowers poked up through the plastic trash of discarded snow fence netting and bamboo poles, adorned with fluorescent tape, and used to mark hazards on the ski runs in winter, now lay discarded in the meadows. Scars from machinery traversing the fragile soil were evident all over; stockpiles of lumber and black plastic water pipe lay in tangled messes. Pieces of metal and tin from various projects lay rusting in the summer sun, and in the air there was the pungent odour of hydraulic fluid, chairlift cable grease and the oil used to lubricate various pieces of equipment. We hiked over to the lower ski runs to gain the meadowland above.

Our first camping spot was at Howard Douglas Lake, six kilometres away. As we ascended through the ski area, Alex saw a beer can in the trailside grass, a flagrant cast off from some snapped–up springtime skier. This can, however, was unopened and he quickly added it to his pack for later consumption. We rambled across the extensive plateau of the Sunshine Meadows which, according to Park literature was part of one of the largest alpine meadow systems in the entire world! That's quite an impressive statement. At over 2200 metres, the extensive views were breathtaking and our eyes feasted upon the infinite array of alpine flowers.

We stopped for lunch and drank our free beer on an outcropping from Quartz Ridge that rises above Howard Douglas Lake. In the far distance, under gathering storm clouds, we could see our objective, Mount Assiniboine. It was shortly after noon and far too early to descend to camp, so we hung our packs in the tree line larches and climbed to the saddle on Quartz Hill. We scampered to the northwest side over jumbled blocks of quartzite, and were treated to a view of the Simpson River valley, thousands of feet below.

Sir George Simpson, the "Little Emperor" of the Hudson Bay Company travelled through the valley in 1841, guided by Indians who had used the corridor for centuries. We could look up the North Fork of the Simpson, known in those days as Teepee Pole Creek to the environs of the pass. In later years it was used by fur trappers such as Bill Peyto and Conrad Kain, and as a pack train route for early exploration trips to Mount Assiniboine led by outfitters like the Brewster brothers and the legendary Tom Wilson. Bill Peyto guided Sir James Outram through here in 1901; the year Outram successfully completed the first ascent of Mount Assiniboine. In subsequent years, other routes were favoured as a means of getting into the Assiniboine area and the Simpson Valley trail fell into disuse.

We sat on the grassy slope and gazed across at Monarch Mountain, Simpson Pass, and Larix, Grizzly and the Healy Lakes sprawled across the larch–studded meadowland opposite. Directly below us, we spied a bachelor group of bighorn rams perhaps twelve in number, some of them grazing, others lying on the tundra grasses, chewing their cud in the warm sun. We sat against a large chunk of quartz and watched them as the sun, shadow, and cloud played across the alpine. In the blue distance we could see Spar Mountain and Mount Verendrye, peaks that soar above the Banff–Radium highway, and in the northwest, Mount Ball and Storm Mountain were still holding on to their winter snow. Closer in I was able to pick out the Monarch Ramparts, where I had hiked the previous summer and Harvey Pass, under Mount Borgeau, another place I had visited that year. As I sat and listened to the land, I thought back to when I had plodded along those trails as the cancer danced through my body. I had been so damn scared then, and so very tired. A mere shadow of my present self. Modern medicine and a positive approach had worked miracles on my shattered soul. Alex moved about, identifying various species of alpine flora for me. I was receiving an education. We were sitting at an elevation of over 2500 metres and the growing season is perhaps only 45 days long. A fine, deep blue sky began to materialize and clouds of brilliant white and dark grey were suspended in the air.

Gradually we circled Quartz Hill, came back to our packs and hoisted our belongings for the descent to the campground on the shores of the little lake. "This is it?" Alex exclaimed with mock dismay as I shook out the tent and enquired how he liked Howard Douglas Lake.

"Yeah man, this is home"! I retorted.

"This isn't going to work," he whined, "I thought you said we were staying at a Howard Johnson's, you know, the hotel chain!" His mirthless chortling had me shaking my head. This might turn into a really long hike! There was one other tent there and we set ours up as the late–evening light blasted across the land from under the heavy cloud cover. Low–angle light in the evening is always so vibrant and intense and arouses the artistic senses in a photographer. As the evening cooled and the shadows deepened, we sat by the still tarn and watched the eastern brook trout feeding on the abundant mosquitoes. I had not hiked with Alex before and so I was quite impressed when he brought forth his double shot of "instant fire." Though it was hard to believe, he had actually packed in a sizeable chunk of "dura–log", which burned with quiet comfort as the light left our valley. The double shot of "instant fire" was revealed when he extracted from his jacket pocket a seething concoction of sambuca and rye whiskey! It burned like fire as it went down and it instantly became my best friend. I packed a small flask of this with me for the rest of the season. It was a fine cap to a great day in the alpine. The flickering flame of the dura–log left us yearning for the earlier times, when campfires were allowed in these areas. Parks Canada had been monitoring this activity for several years. Blackened fire circles in too many different locations, along with a scarcity of wood in the alpine had put an end to this evening comfort.

I eased out of my tent early the next morning and checked in on Alex, who was resting peacefully in an open–ended tent fly. He looked like he would be out for another couple of hours and as the other tent was quiet as well, I went over to the lake for an early morning wash. The dawn blue was quickly being replaced by some high cirrus cresting across the divide on the wings of a westerly breeze. The green waters of the lake reflected the clouds as they crowded in along the skyline.

Gradually the camp came to life and we ate our breakfast, before assembling our possessions and embarking on the trail to

Og Lake, sixteen kilometres away. As we moved across the rich meadows below Citadel Pass, Alex, who was perhaps 20 metres behind, captured my attention with a softly spoken entreaty. "Hey buddy, shhhh, check this out," he whispered. Just by his tone, I thought I knew what he had seen. Having been a Kananaskis park ranger in years past, he had been talking bears almost incessantly on this trip. If I had ever wanted to see a grizz back here in the woods, this would be the guy with whom I would like to share the excitement.

I backed up and followed Alex's pointed finger. "Holy shit, you found a bear," I enthused. Off to the right, in some willow shin–tangle, a bear stood watching us, unprovoked but getting more curious by the second. He was about 60 metres from us, far too close for comfort. He was obviously a grizzly; a chocolate, subadult with a pronounced shoulder hump.

With the adrenaline coursing through my body, I couldn't decide whether I should grab the camera or grab the bear spray, so I did neither; I just let my senses take in the event. His furry ears twitched and his beady eyes were fixed on us. Alex guessed it was a boar. Had it been a sow, he reasoned, or worse, a sow with cubs at heel, we would have been far too close to her. An instant charge would have been the only appropriate response for a protective mother bear. We smart backpackers had apparently blundered right into this bear's territory. We watched for only 20 seconds before he became agitated and started moving around. Initially I think, he had been content to let us pass, but as soon as we stopped, he became alert. The bear quartered slightly left, dropped his head, then climbed up on a fallen larch, presumably to get a better view. We decided perhaps we should take our leave, and once behind a screen of Englemann spruce trees, we hustled away. For the next few metres, we peered cautiously over our shoulders as we headed up towards Citadel Pass.

We were not yet two hours into the hike, and already the day had taken on a sharp edge. We looked at each other and knew we had just been given a fantastic gift. Alex was beside himself with excitement and happiness, and after the adrenaline had pumped down a notch or two, so was I. It had been a truly magnificent encounter, the quintessential wilderness experience that all hikers dream about. It was indeed fortunate for us that the bear had not been aggressive or excitable. We were ecstatic; we felt privileged; we had a memory that would last a lifetime.

Alex and I rested on Citadel Pass for a bit and ate some GORP. We were on the Continental Divide, at 2360 metres and about to leave Banff National Park and Alberta and enter Mount Assiniboine Provincial Park in British Columbia. We started down toward the Porcupine campground and upon entering the forest noticed some grizzly bear diggings. As they appeared rather recent, we kept a watchful eye out and made some noise from time to time. Then a bit farther along, we saw some scat, which looked quite fresh, and as we moved further down into the valley, we encountered more evidence of recent excavation. Vast areas immediately adjacent to the trail had recently been torn up in an attempt to harvest the hedysarum root bulb. In some places, the excavated dirt had been thrown right across the trail; the sod and ripped grasses and flowers looked as if they had just landed! This indeed was very fresh sign. Most recent, according to my park ranger friend.

We now became very alert and cautious. We were quite on edge. There was no one around to help us if we should run into trouble. The next three kilometres were full of blind corners and 8–metre sightlines. We were in deep forest and our nerves were dancing. Alex took pictures of one dig, six metres long, and two metres wide, with the dirt still settling on the leaves. We walked around several piles of scats, two of which still retained some heat. Alex said he had not seen activity on this scale before. In fact, he thought perhaps there was more than one bear about. Hundreds of square yards of mountain vegetation had been ripped asunder by the ursine desire to fill the ole' belly. The last hour in this valley had certainly provided an education as well as a fascinating, albeit heart racing experience. I sure as hell know now what fresh bear sign really looks like!

Gradually we were able to vacate the feeding area. Sight lines improved and we rested for a spell on the grassy slope above the Porcupine Campground. I mentioned to Alex that I was surprised how few hikers were back here; we hadn't seen a soul all day and it is a very popular hiking route. It was almost as if the trail had been closed. With the kind of imminent bear activity we had just experienced, I could understand the Park closing this section of the trail, but that couldn't possibly be the case because we had not seen a trail closure sign up on Citadel Pass.

We moved on into the Golden Valley and I thought back to the last time I was there, with Cecilia in 1983. I remembered how thirsty and dehydrated we had become because of a lack of water and the incredible heat. The trail literature of the time had warned hikers about the dryness of the area; the karst topography ensured that most surface water drained underground and there was no reliable water source between Citadel Pass and Og Lake. We were aware of this, but had drunk all our water on this very hot day in the Golden Valley. Initially, we were not concerned as we were each carrying three oranges. When we grabbed the oranges to suck on we found that they were all rotten inside and inedible. No fluid nourishment for us! By the time we arrived at Og Lake, we felt like we were on our last legs. The extreme heat and dehydration had sapped all our strength. I remember that I stripped all my clothes off and jumped right into the lake, sank to the bottom and then opened my mouth!

On this late afternoon, as Alex and I threaded our way through the Valley of the Rocks, a fierce hailstorm moved through the basin. It lasted for a long time and soaked us thoroughly before it moved on over Og Mountain. We reached the Og Lake Campground just as a rain shower swept into camp. This is a dreary, desolate place in this kind of weather. The tent sites are located among the willow bushes with no sheltering trees for a hundred metres. On our arrival we noticed one other tent sitting alone on a gravel bench below.

There is no fresh water either, the distant lake the only source and that by definition is suspect. The lake is nothing more than a catch basin and the water cannot be trusted. We had been hiking for over eight hours and had travelled over 16 kilometres It was another seven kilometres to the comfortable camp at Lake Magog, but we just didn't have the resolve; we were wet, tired and hungry.

I erected the tent between showers and Alex devised a fly for us to cook under. In due course we heated up some dinner and felt a little better. To the south, Mount Assiniboine, Mount Magog and Terrapin Mountain stood under a grey and foreboding sky. We drank some hot tea and talked. Alex proved to be a very relaxed and knowledgeable hiking partner. During the day, he had shown me many plants that were new to me. In addition I knew all I needed to about the hedysarum plant; it was a member of the pea family, and bears will rip all the dirt from the face of the earth, if need be, to get at it!

In the late evening, Alex went up on a high bench behind camp to catch the fleeting rays of the evening sun as it sank beneath the peaks while I took a stroll down toward the lake. I saw a sign by the trail and went over to investigate. In official, bold red and blue it read, "Danger, trail closed, bear in area!" It advised hikers of the trail closure between Assiniboine and Sunshine meadows. There had not been a similar sign at Citadel Pass; if there had been one our trip would have been cancelled. All right, I nodded to myself, that was why we had not seen any hikers coming toward us that day. We had been fortunate to pass the area of bear activity without incident and I was glad to have had a hiking companion and an extra set of eyes that day.

I sat in some mountain heather above the lake and thought again about "our" bear. A poem, Grizzly, by Graeme Pole came to mind.

I bring to this meeting
My belief that I will not encounter you;
That I am immune to the threat of your presence.
After all, it's been three years now
And we are yet to meet.
Thus in ignorance I walk onto your ground
Without even the courtesy of making noise
To let you know that I am here.

You bring to this meeting
The knowledge that perhaps within a few decades
Your kind will no longer dwell here;
Driven from these valleys and meadows
By those whose fear demands blood,
To the only solitude remaining - eternity.

I see your shoulder come through the trees
Fur and muscle rippling in the sun
A beauty so primal.
And I see in your eyes
The dismay of all your kind
And of all the others of the land, air, and water
Who have vanished before you.

I am aware that you could take my life in an instant.
But I wonder at this moment
Who of us is really the most afraid.
For I also see the reality of that which each of us is defending.

Though fear of meeting you is my greatest concern
   in these mountains
I do not curse you, grizzly.
Nor wish that you live any other place
Nor travel any other trails
Than those do I.

We were lucky, the day could have turned out differently. The personality of the bruin choreographed the scene. How many times over the years have I failed to see wildlife as I passed through their homes? I have little doubt that I have travelled by all manner of animals that I would have been overjoyed to see, but had not been attuned to their presence, my "city senses" robbing me of these encounters. I do feel that I am an alert hiker and I always watch the trail ahead, just as one watches the highway. What is off to the side is just that; out of the picture. That day, without an extra set of eyes, I would have missed a most profound experience.

Back in the tent as darkness and another shower dropped into our valley, Alex started chuckling. "Ya know that other tent over there? The guy came out and gave me Hell," he said. Alex went on to relate that, unbeknownst to him, a woman from that tent had gone down to the lake, stripped down to the buff and waded in for a cooling bath. The guy had come out of his tent to see how she was doing and, upon gazing about the hills, noticed Alex up there looking in her direction with what appeared to be, a damn fine set of binoculars! In truth, Alex could not see her because of a intervening rib of rock and knew nothing of the situation whatsoever. As Alex came back down through camp, this fellow, a visiting German, accosted him and said something about Alex watching his lady taking a bath. Alex was able to convince him that it was not binoculars, but rather a camera he had with him; why it didn't even have a telephoto lens! The guy apologized, "Ach, dat is not dey shhpyglas!" Alex affected a solemn pose and informed the gentleman that he was camped at *Og Lake*, not *Oggle Lake*. I didn't bother to tell Alex that I, on the other side of the lake, had not been so encumbered with an "intervening rib of rock." He might have seen Ursus, but I also had sharp eyes!

~

A cool, grey dawn greeted me as I crawled from the tent and into the chilly air. It had showered on and off during the night and, with a very low ceiling, there was not much to see of our surroundings. We rounded up our belongings and marched out of camp toward the campground at Lake Magog. Today we had but seven kilometres of travel and we knew that we would be at the lake by noon, so we diverted from the trail to explore a nearby cave we had seen the night before. This area of the park also has a karst topography. Much of the surface water here, including most of the lakes, drains underground through cave systems in the soft limestone. The cave we investigated was about 40 metres above the trail. Once inside, we saw it was quite spacious, about four metres high and 15 metres deep. In poor weather, it would be a serviceable shelter.

As we hiked over the meadows near Lake Magog to our camp, the weather closed in. The final kilometre was a dash to beat the oncoming rain, a race that we lost. We set our tent up in the first available spot and sat under a tree to wait out the shower. Two hours later, the rain let up and we explored the camp, looking for a more pleasing tent site, which we eventually found. We returned to our site and lifted the tent up between us and with our packs on, paraded through the camp to our new quarters. There were several fellow hikers here and as we shuffled through, one of these characters hollered over to us, "Say rookies, didja know those damn tents will fold right down, you can actually jam'em in yer pack!" We heard a few guffaws. The joke was on us, and I guess we did look a bit silly.

Later that afternoon, we walked over to Mount Assiniboine Lodge, which is situated above the lake, in hopes of finding Sepp. He and his wife Barb ran the lodge and had extensive knowledge of the area. Sepp Renner was a former ski and mountain guide and has climbed Mount Assiniboine over 30 times. Alex wanted to query him about routes up the mountain, as he thought he would go on up to the Hind Hut on a reconnaissance mission the next day. Sepp wasn't around, but one of the staff provided Alex with a route book for him to peruse.

We left and meandered over to the Naiset Cabins. These log structures are looked after by B.C. Provincial Parks and are reserved on a first come, first served basis. With this inclement weather, they were chock full. The cabins were built in 1924 by A. O. Wheeler, a surveyor with the Interprovincial Boundary Commission. He used them for his "Walking Tours." The venture only lasted two years. He then sublet the property to Marquis Albizzi, a winter sports director from New York. Albizzi envisioned a ski area here and, in 1928, he and Erling Strom took the first guests into the area for the purpose of skiing. It was so successful that the partners asked the Canadian Pacific Railway to build a lodge there. They said they could keep the lodge going winter and summer and the CPR, always on the lookout for new promotional activities, agreed. Erling Strom ran this lodge until his retirement in 1975. Mount Assiniboine Lodge is now privately run under lease from the B.C. Provincial Government, while the Naiset cabins are managed by the resident Park Ranger.

We walked over to the ranger cabin to talk with Allen, the Park Ranger on duty. Alex mentioned to him that he had once been employed with the Alberta Provincial Parks branch, over in the Kananaskis area. They had a good palaver on the front porch. Allen was interested in our bear–sighting and subsequent viewing of the bear activity around Citadel Pass. He was a little concerned that we had chosen to come through on the "closed" trail, but we were able to convince him that his warden buddies over in Banff had not "signed" their end of the trail.

We stood on his porch and waited out yet another passing shower before heading over to our tent for dinner. On the way back to camp, we saw a solitary hiker coming along, hunched over in the misty rain. As he got closer, I thought perhaps I'd seen him somewhere before. When he closed in on our position, he looked up and grinned, "Jeez, haven't seen you since Egypt!" Why, it was Hank, the guy who had given me that fuel canister and all that extra GORP at Egypt Lake three weeks ago! We talked briefly and invited him over to the tent later on for an evening confab.

The heavy cloud induced a premature twilight and by the time we had cooked our dinner and cleaned up the camp, night was almost upon us. Alex got his dura–log going just as Hank came into our camp. Under the fly, with the ambience of the fake–fire and the pattering rain, we brewed up some tea and swapped yarns.

Hank was, it turned out, a marathon runner and was travelling very light on this trip into "th' boine," as he called it. In one day and out the next, he explained. His pack contained a sleeping bag, tent fly, rain jacket, and some GORP to munch. He had been able to cover the 30 kilometres from the Mount Shark trailhead in under six hours. He was heading back early the next morning to his car, and then going home to Stettler, 350 kilometres away.

After he left, we just shook our heads. It was hard for us to understand how anyone could come into such a beautiful area like this and be in such a rush. He was like a whirling dervish; he had to keep moving, keep on the go. His demeanour, his *raison d' etre* was, to us, all wrong. On this, our third day, we were just happily adjusting to the mountain mystique, why we *never* wanted to go back. Yet it seemed he couldn't wait to return home. However, in fairness, we understood that his reasons for coming in here were far different than ours. He was a long distance runner and fitness buff; to him this was simply more training. As another shower came into camp, we jumped into our bags and discussed our plans for the next day. Alex wanted to go up to the Hind Hut, on the lower slopes of Mount Assiniboine, if the weather was decent. I thought I would visit some of the local attractions at a much lower elevation.

~

Dawn came to Mount Assiniboine in the grandest fashion. After the previous day's showery weather, we were delighted to rise to morning sunshine and a sky of cobalt blue. I fairly tripped over myself as I hustled out of the dark confines of the forest campground and into the dazzling meadowland above the shores of Lake Magog, my camera ready for action. The dew on the grass sparkled like a million diamonds reflecting the morning sunlight and with the simple magnificence of the peak above, the whole scene appeared dreamlike. Mount Assiniboine stood sharply defined against a sky of azure blue, its familiar cloud bonnet streaming out from the summit ice cap. This mountain has surprised and enchanted me so many times in recent years.

I came back to camp to find Alex hunkered over his stove, preparing his morning meal. He was as keen as I was to get going and explore this dazzling environment. I walked with him as far as the end of the lake and then turned back as he ascended the talus fan above, en route to the Hind Hut. He was not sure what lay ahead for him; he was optimistic enough to believe he might in fact climb Assiniboine if reasonable conditions and available mountaineers presented themselves. If that happened, we agreed that he would not come back to our tent before noon the next day. If he was unable to find anyone to climb with, he might rock scramble on one of the nearby peaks, such as Strom, Lunette or Sturdee; or he might run into poor weather and be back in camp by mid–afternoon.

I tidied up the campsite, then left for a solitary ramble over to the nearby lakes, Sunburst, Cerulean and Elizabeth. I poked around Lizzie Rummel's old cabin at Sunburst Lake; it was still useable though at present it was shuttered and locked. It had originally been built for Pat Brewster in 1937, before he turned it over to Lizzie around 1950. There was a cold–storage room built into an adjacent hillside, complete with mortared rock and a sturdy door, still serviceable as well. Beyond was a firewood–gathering area, and some felled trees waiting to be bucked up on an improvised sawhorse frame. These days, the cabin is used mainly by trail maintenance crews hired on a seasonal basis by the provincial parks. Some of their duties include removing downed trees from the trails, spreading gravel on paths that were experiencing problems with erosion, painting trail signs and general cleaning.

I hiked over to Cerulean Lake and on up to Elizabeth Lake. It was nice being there by myself, though I wondered idly where everyone was. I was sure there were at least 40 people at the lodge, maybe as many as 30 at the Naiset cabins and another 20 or 30 souls in the campground, yet here I was on my own, enjoying one of the finest days in the past while. I backtracked and climbed a ridge on the Nub and, on topping out shortly after noon, I found several hikers enjoying the view. Coming off the summit of the Nub, I counted 18 hikers descending to the trees, it was now getting almost too crowded!

The wildflower displays were astonishing and included fleabane, arnica, paintbrush and anemone. I investigated various photo angles. The paintbrush, with their varied hues, ranging from vermilion and salmon to pale yellow, were particularly attractive. As I took some frames, I talked with a like–minded individual who was staying over at the lodge. He told me that three weeks previously Sepp, while hiking in this vicinity with a large group, had surprised a grizzly about ten metres away in the bush. Normally, one would think, a grizzly would bolt from such a noisy bunch, but not this bear. Bears in our parks are gradually becoming aware of increased hiker traffic through their home ranges. It would be a mistake, however, to think they are adapting or changing their behaviour because of us. Bears are, by their very nature, completely unpredictable. While it may be said that they are losing their natural fear of us, they certainly will retain their aggressive personalities; that is an intrinsic part of being a bear. A warden once said to me, "We have National Parks to protect our wild animals, but with so many hikers in the backcountry, how do we keep the "wild" in these animals?"

After taking some pictures, I hiked down to the lodge, sat by a stream, washed my socks and soaked my feet before walking slowly back to the campground in the afternoon sun. On the way, I noted the young fir and spruce in the meadows beside the lake were suffering from some affliction that was turning their needles a rust colour. Closer inspection revealed that these needles were in fact dead and I wondered if the trees themselves would survive. I later discovered that these trees had succumbed to the harsh environment of the previous winter. Normally, in the winter, there is two to three metres of snow blanketing the ground and providing the needed insulation for these small trees, but this past winter, there was barely one metre of snow cover. Because these young spruce and fir did not have the requisite insulation from the snow pack, they had been exposed to the vagaries of severe temperature changes and that, along with the winter winds, had caused irreversible damage.

Later in the afternoon, after hydrating some chili for dinner, I went down to a height of land above the lake to watch Mount Assiniboine change with the afternoon light, write in my journal, and enjoy the breeze that was keeping those damn mosquitoes away. With the showery conditions of the past few days, the bugs had been far from our minds, but today, in the hot sun, they were back, and seemed to have a bad attitude! I was beginning to think they had gone to school with the Baker Lake Boys!

Back in camp, a mule deer came over to the tent to sniff about and keep me company for dinner. She seemed very tame and her soft, liquid eyes watched me as I spooned my chilli. She stayed for about ten minutes, never more than a few paces from where I sat.

Alex returned later that evening. His had been a most rewarding day; he had enjoyed the super weather in the alpine basins beneath Mount Assiniboine. He had been able to kick snow steps up an icy arête to the summit of Mount Strom. As he was pretty done in and, as the bugs continued to torment us, we decided an early night was in order.

~

It was a miserable, wet night in the campground as a cold rain moved in from the west. The chill of a grey dawn had surprised most of us hikers as the previous day had been so grand, but that's what hiking and camping in these mountains is all about. We were, after all, camped on the Continental Divide, under the highest mountain for many miles around. Mount Assiniboine had always been the architect of its own microclimate.

Alex and I decided that we would try to stay in the Naiset Cabins for a night, if space was obtainable. It was pouring rain in the campground and all our stuff was starting to get wet. The cabins were two kilometres closer to the start of the trail to Marvel Pass, and it would also give us a chance to dry some of our equipment. So, after breakfast that morning, we had packed up and headed over to the cabins. They were very full, everyone wanting to stay out of the inclement weather, however we were able to muscle our way in with a family of four from Quebec. Each of the five cabins will sleep eight people, though with that number inside, the cabin begins to resemble a tin and you, well, you become a sardine!

In the 1970s, the B.C. Provincial Government refurbished the Naiset Cabins with wood stoves and new roofs and they now rent them out to skiers and hikers. We spent part of the day at our cabin, the Aster, drying and resorting our gear, then we set off for afternoon tea at Assiniboine Lodge. We spent a happy two hours at the lodge, appreciating the warm and spacious comfort and talking briefly with Sepp and Barb, still the friendly, congenial hosts I remembered from my last visit, three years ago.

As we sat inside the Renner's log abode enjoying hot tea and fresh baked goods, Alex and I went through their library. With the rain rattling on the windowpanes, I looked through a book on the area by Don Beers. Under his description of Marvel Pass, Don includes a picture of an old log structure on the shores of Cabin

Lake. This photo captured my imagination because I had often thought about hiking in this remote corner of Banff Park. I passed the book over to Alex with the suggestion that we try to find this Cabin Lake, wherever it might be. Our original hiking plan had not included Marvel Pass, as it was a few kilometres out of the way. Few backpackers venture in that direction, so we knew the area would be beautiful and wild. We thought we would talk with the ranger that evening and get current information on trails and camping spots.

With tea finished, we tramped back to the Naiset Cabins, but not before Alex, with something up his sleeve, had procured three beers from Sepp. These, he informed me, were keys to the inner sanctum of the nearby ranger station. Things, as previously mentioned, were pretty tight over at our Aster home and Alex intended to relax on the less crowded porch of the ranger cabin after dinner.

As it so happened, Allen was glad to see us. He had some more questions he wanted to ask about our experience with the bear near Citadel Pass. He had filed a report with his supervisors concerning our sighting of the bear and they told him to find those hikers and get some more information. With typical bureaucratic buck passing, his superiors wanted to know exactly where the bear had been spotted. It was hard for us, and to a certain extent their "man in the field," Allen, to comprehend. Really, what did it matter? There was a bear around, let's just deal with it. But these desk jockeys, these government minions, needed to know more facts. Was, for instance, the bear in British Columbia or Alberta when it had first been spotted? If it was in Alberta, it was in Banff National Park and therefore a federal government concern. If, however it was across the divide in B.C., it was in a B.C. Provincial Park and fell under the auspices of the Provincial Government, unless it was in transit from Kootenay National Park, ball now back in the federal court! Should National Park Wardens and federal biologists be notified, or should Provincial Park Rangers be alerted, along with the provincial arm of the Fish and Wildlife department? Alex and I just shook our heads and sipped our beers; by the time these cowboys got things figured out, the bear will have died from old age!

I was reminded of one of the old time wardens, Bill Neish, who many years ago had been forced to keep a daily log on his warden activities in Banff Park, at the behest of the dominion government. While recording events in a proper fashion was part and parcel of the job, it rankled most of these weathered old timers to have to account for their daily movements throughout their assigned districts. "The less the `Dumb–Onion gument' knew, the better"! Anyway, there was one entry in his warden journal that eventually ended up in Ottawa, as all warden journals did, and caused some bureaucrat to raise his eyebrows and straighten his tie with astonishment. Part of the tersely written entry read, "hunting bandits three hours." Ottawa sent back a reply as quickly as was possible in those days, a request for a full and proper accounting of the entire event. It fell to old Bill to expand on his diary entry. He wrote back giving the government all the expanded information that he felt they needed: Jim Deegan's poem sums it up.

In Ottawa, the Parks' Director
who liked things trim and neat
received Bill's monthly diary.
The information was incomplete.

When asked for further particulars
which Bill didn't like too well,
he grabbed a pencil and scribbled—
"It was snowing like blooming Hell!"

It was true then and it is true now: these guys back in the office, far removed from the scent of pine trees and saddle leather, simply cannot comprehend what it's like back in the bush.

Allen graciously asked us inside his palace. It was an extremely well–built ranger cabin, made of sound logs and a properly finished interior. It contained a loft with two bedrooms and had large picture windows fronting the porch. It was very different from any backcountry ranger station I had ever seen. Allen explained that the previous cabin had burned down one winter a few years back and, as luck would have it, there was a surplus of cash in the provincial coffers when bids came in to build new accommodations.

Alex, with his past experience as a ranger was of the opinion that parks personnel did not need this kind of luxury when back in the woods on patrol. It was better, he believed, to have a small cabin, easy to clean, maintain and heat. I however, felt that to visitors who had travelled to this place from around the world, a solid, beautiful log cabin in the Canadian wilds showed the government's commitment to the stewardship and protection of our national scenic wealth. With the Canadian and British Columbia flags waving gaily on a nearby flagpole, their colours in vivid contrast to the deep green forest, I felt sure the log structure would instill an unforgettable picture of strength and pride in many a visitor.

In the amicable atmosphere of this grand mountain lair, we three enjoyed a great chinwag as the showers continued outside and a cool wind moaned in the chimney piping. While we sipped on our beers Allen, who was on active duty and not able to accept our frothy libation, regaled us with information on the area from behind a large pot of tea. Alex and Allen set tentative plans for a possible climb of Mount Assiniboine. Allen had ascended the mountain from the south a year earlier, and wanted to climb it again, this time using the normal route of ascent, the northeast ridge. We asked Allen if he knew anything about the trail to Marvel Pass. He said he had been through there before, though, as it was in Banff Park, it was not now part of his jurisdiction. He said it was "prime" country and we took that to mean it was special, and worth seeing. When I asked him if that was what he had meant, he said, "Oh yeah, definitely worth a visit, hardly anyone goes back there, its prime grizzly country. You really want to watch yourselves back there!" Alex's eyes lit up like a kid's at Christmas, I just shook my head and rolled my eyes; but secretly I knew I would be in for some fun. In truth, I doubt I would have gone over Marvel Pass if I had been on my own, but with a fellow hiker, I was ready and keen.

We thanked Allen for his help and hospitality and headed back to our dark den. The air was very cool and we were happy to be inside for the night. The cabin was black as midnight in a mineshaft, and we had to feel around as best we could, trying not to make any noise that would disturb our Quebeçois friends. We were on the upper berth and the roof log rafters were within inches of my nose as I lay in my bag. I couldn't see them, but I felt them with my hand. Sitting bolt upright from a bad dream was not an option that night!

~

I arose in the soft grey light of dawn and stepped outside. My unlaced boots crunched across the wooden porch decking and while neither one of my eyes seemed ready to function, my mind numbly registered the crunching sound, and I wondered, "now what the heck is that?" About that time I skidded right off the porch, missed the first step, hammered off the second, and skated to the gravel path, arms windmilling about me. Now my eyes were wide open! Snow!, Jeez it's snow! More correctly, there was icy sleet underfoot, but snow in the grass and on the tree branches. It was July the 25 and as I gazed over at Mount Cautley, I thought that it would make a credible ski hill; why, it was plastered from summit to tree line with a dazzling white coat of fresh snow. Boy, the weather in the alpine, I thought to myself. At least the mosquitoes were done with, for a bit!

With our stomachs full of porridge, hydrated strawberries and warm coffee, Alex and I were on the trail bright and early and up at Wonder Pass in an hour and a half. The pass itself was breezy and cool, but the sun was trying to get into the picture. Far to the north, we could see Citadel Peak, and farther on, the ski hills, dusted with snow, at Sunshine Village. With some regret we turned our backs on Mount Assiniboine and started our steep descent to the shores of Marvel Lake, 600 metres below.

While we could see across the valley to the environs of Marvel Pass, we were not sure of the route, so we took a sighting on the meadowland near the pass before dropping down into the forest. Tiny Terrapin Lake and the much larger Gloria Lake winked at us through the trees as we descended. These lakes, along with Marvel, acquire the most stunning colours of aqua blue and emerald green when seen from the sub–alpine slopes hundreds of metres above. Helicopter flights carrying tourists converge on this area all day long in the summer, their constant clatter an intrusive annoyance to the backpacker. The rides last about 15 minutes and originate in Canmore, just outside the park. The helicopters fly directly over the lakes, then swing in under the glaciers and ice fields on Mount Eon and Mount Aye before swooping back down to the distant Bow Valley.

The forest became jungle–dense as we neared the shores of Marvel Lake. It is a very damp local environment with the three bodies of water in the valley and glaciers ringing the southern and western walls. It was very dark and quiet in there, the canopy closed in over our heads filtering out most of the available light. The inlet stream that cascades down from Gloria Lake had taken out the log bridge some time in the past and we were forced to cross the creek through water up to our knees. Once across, we were happy to find a well defined trail leading up into the sub–alpine.

On the way up the trail, I noticed a diamond–shaped carving, perhaps eight inches on each side, on the trunk of a large fir. Somebody, at one time, had spent a couple of hours chopping the bark from the tree in order to fashion some sort of message. Closer inspection revealed the pencil scrawl preserved in sap "Bill Vroom, on way by horse to Owl Lake, 1970." This warden, from Banff Park had travelled this way 31 years ago. By happenstance I knew this guy; in fact my first stirrings of interest in a career as a park warden were probably because of this man. In 1965 I had been a volunteer ski patroller at Sunshine Village, and that ski area was part of Billy's district. We would meet him at his cabin on Healy Creek with our skis and youthful enthusiasm, and he would have the green Jeep J20 warming up outside in the frosty morning air. We'd all pile in and head up to Sunshine Village on the fire road. As I was an impressionable 18–year old with only two years of driving under my belt, this was indeed, a mighty heady experience for me. It was a cool road to drive on with lots of twists and turns over the steep, snowcovered surface, and we were in a four–wheel drive half–ton to boot! Here was this affable man, so obviously enjoying his mountains, his job, and that nifty cabin back in the woods—why he was larger than life to me and he had the coolest park issue fur–skin hat made out of a beaver hide. We would get up to the patrol cabin at the village and he would go inside to get a fire going in the stove. After a bit he would come out to ski and assign duties to us novice patrollers. He was mild mannered and always had any number of fascinating warden stories to tell. I was enthralled by his account of the cougar he saw while on horseback. Man, a cougar! Think of that! Or the visit by a wolverine to one of his backcountry patrol cabins. I was into reading Outdoor Life magazines in those days and I loved to hear his stories; looking back, he was a hero to me. I knew I wanted to be just like him; he got to ride a horse through these beautiful peaks and crags and carried a rifle in a scabbard on his saddle. I definitely wanted to become a park warden, to sit up in the woods in a log cabin, to go out and ski in virgin powder snow....

Over the years, I'd hear of Bill Vroom from time to time as he ascended through the park bureaucracy. Reader's Digest did a good story on him in 1973 and I still have it in my library. During the 1950s and 1960s, a man named Walter Perren was charged with forming a mountain rescue team out of warden service personnel in response to a substantial increase in mountain climbing accidents. Now, sticking your feet into crampons instead of stirrups was a whole new concept to these cowboys, but Billy Vroom proved to be a quick study and rose immediately to the challenges of the new technologies. Bill soon became very adept and well respected in this field. He gained high recognition in park management and at the time of his retirement was the Backcountry Supervisor for the southern half of Banff National Park.

These thoughts preoccupied me as I climbed the remaining 200 metres up into the alpine environs of Marvel Pass. I found my hiking partner up there, stretched out in the grass, half–asleep in the noonday sun. We lost the sketchy trail a few times but it seemed of no concern as every step we took revealed new and exciting details. We set our packs down near a small pond and rambled at will across the rocky plateau. We were enchanted with the rolling grasses and rocky buttresses and there were several shallow tarns to explore. A great fire had swept through the area many years ago, leaving giant snags of every conceivable shape and size. The weathered log carcasses lay on the heath and were festooned with a colourful assortment of mountain flora while others stood in bleached and gnarled shapes that twisted towards the sky. We continued to explore this high playground, traversing through copses of larch trees and by mossy seeps of gorgeous green. Eventually we climbed a boulder outcropping and stared down into the valley of Aurora Creek far below as it wound its way down to the Mitchell River in B.C. We sat there for half an hour, all alone, nobody about for miles it seemed. "We're sure up in the high lonesome now, buddy," Alex remarked as we took in range after range of mountains that faded in the blue and hazy distance.

We didn't have much of a map, and there was no defined trail at this point. "Do you suppose this is the pass," I wondered aloud. "Because if it's Marvel Pass, we must be back in B.C. now." We had left B.C. earlier when we crested the Continental Divide at Wonder Pass. The trail descended form the pass into Banff Park and Alberta. We did not really care where we were, it was just so good to be there; the weather, though cloudy, was stable and the day was warm. There was a ridge rising behind us to the east but as there was no break or obvious route, we had no reason to suspect Marvel Pass was over there. "I'm wondering, do you think maybe that Cabin Lake is on the other side of that ridge, Alex?" I still had Cabin Lake on the brain; I really wanted to see it. So we decided to check it out, our packs were about two kilometres behind us, back by one of the lakes. It looked like a 40 minute scramble up to the ridge; the day was yet young, and if nothing else, we'd get a splendid view.

We climbed up through the trees and abruptly crested out onto the shores of a peaceful, quiet lake. Immediately we saw the cabin on the opposite shore, five feet from the water up against a grove of larch trees. We were standing beside the tiny outlet stream and at our feet was an old rock–rimmed fire circle. We looked at each other and knew that this was home for the night; it was so tranquil and picturesque. We had intersected a bit of a trail as we came up through the trees and we now felt we were "back on track", to use a bad pun.

It was closing in on supper hour and we were getting pretty ravenous, so we hustled back down to the little lake to retrieve our packs. Working our way across the upper reaches of the plateau, we noticed several bear digs and reasoned that he was after the nutrient–rich glacier lily bulb. The whole area of this open forest was carpeted with glacier lilies, as was the adjacent meadow.

We climbed back up through the trees very slowly, our packs were starting to sap our quickly depleting energy. Near the lake we came across some fresh bear scat. "Hmmph, so they *are* around here somewhere," we thought. We got to the fire circle and dumped our packs on the soft lakeshore moss, stretched out our sore backs and congratulated ourselves on a superb wilderness camp. "And we're going to have a fire," Alex enthused., "There's no one else around; we have a ready made fire pit, and lots of dry wood nearby. Man it's going to be great up here!"

As I looked around for a flat spot on which to erect the tent, Alex went searching for some kindling. His, "Oh shit man, look at this," wasn't what I wanted to hear at that time of day. I went over to check out his findings and discovered a large area of freshly–dug shoreline real estate. An area perhaps 30 metres by ten metres had been uprooted by Mr. Ursine Excavator who, it would appear, enjoyed a view while he dined! We felt these diggings to be less than a day old by the way the loosely clumped soil fell off leaves and grass stems. The area looked very similar to ones garden after it has been freshly spaded. The small opening in the trees by the outlet stream was a natural wildlife corridor to this lake. Logically, it would be used as an entrance and exit route by all animals in the vicinity. Now, with fresh bear sign nearby, it would appear to be pure stupidity to set up the tent right in the middle of this animal passageway. Where to go now? Maybe camping by this lake wasn't such a hot idea. We exchanged grins and shrugged our shoulders and moved over to investigate the cabin. It was a roofless, doorless contrivance and the weathered logs appeared to be quite ancient; probably some old trappers cabin from an earlier era.

We sat with our backs against the sun–bleached log walls and appreciated the late afternoon sun as it shimmered off the lake. It was about six pm and we were starved. Dinner was the first order of business, and we contemplated setting up camp by the cabin. As I got the stove roaring and some fresh lake water in the pot, Alex went off to inspect the area behind the cabin. He came back with a bit of dry wood for the proposed fire and a grim expression on his face. "Man, we're surrounded. You should see the bear diggings back there." We went back and it looked as if a bomb had gone off! The bear, or bears, had dug and ripped furiously through the turf in their continuous quest for more nutrients and protein.

We moved quietly down to the lakeshore, half–expecting to see a furry brown hide behind the next tree. I looked down into the still water of the little bay and saw three clods of soil and moss floating on the surface. Now just how recent was this? How long should it take for them to sink, or break apart? My mind conjured up the bear, his nose in the lilies and his rump up in the air, hanging over the lake, front claws scooping and ejecting these missiles between his hind legs to soar end over end out into the lake.

Alex did some detective work in one area and was able to barely discern the imprint of a paw in the dry dirt. Some of the soil was damp, while other parts were drying in the late sun which led him to believe this site had been revisited. With such an extensive area having been harvested, Alex, with his training, decided there was more than one bear about, possibly a sow with cubs. He also believed they were not just passing through; they were here for awhile, apparently returning to previous dig sites.

Back in camp, sitting hunched over our soup, we went over our options. Neither one of us wanted to stay there that night. It was just way too close to an active grizzly bear feeding area. But, we had hiked about 12 kilometres, and wandered about on the plateau for perhaps another three. Our round trip to pick up our packs was another two kilometres. We were three hours away from pitch dark and Owl Lake was a distant nine kilometres.

Draining the last dregs of his soup, Alex shrugged and said, "You know, I was in Kananaskis for five years, and I saw lots of bears and their dig sites, but I never saw anything like this before. This has got to be one hungry bear, to chew the countryside up like this." I suggested maybe we should go on down to Owl, it was pretty much downhill all the way, and if we got going right now, we'd be down before full dark. But both of us gazed out over the lake with late evening shadows playing across the tranquil surface. We didn't want to leave, it was just so peaceful. We needed to draw the line, the fine line between common sense and an overactive imagination. I wanted to defer to Alex's better understanding of the situation. He said it was dangerous here, camping in a bear's feeding area. Common sense in me agreed, but was it not possible the bear was far away, perhaps in another valley? Suppose Ursus was down on the avalanche slopes above Owl Lake this evening and we go traipsing down there as dark falls on the land, just as the cool air entices the bruin to come out and forage. It came down to one of those intangible questions to which there was no black and white, no clear cut answer. Stay, go, it didn't matter, fate would decide what was in store for us.

In the end Alex and I felt we both knew two things for sure; one: that we were too bone weary to travel any farther. Two: bears were not in the habit of stalking hikers. So we decided to stay. An incredible late–evening glow began to spread across the alpine meadows above the lake. It was our plan to walk around in this beautiful environment for an hour or so, hopefully leaving our scent everywhere we visited. Then, as darkness fell, we would return and build up a great fire against the evening chill. The smoke, we reasoned, would dissipate throughout the valley and any forest creature about would become aware of something different in their neighbourhood.

Wandering around that evening in the warm tangerine glow of the setting sun remains one of the most poignant memories of that summer. We felt so removed from the trappings of civilization; we were alone, there were no other hikers in this valley. The ancient fire–killed trees stood as silent sentinels against a darkening sky that was busy ushering in the first stars. We were close to tree line, in the last refuge of the larches with just a breath of wind filtering through. Cabin Lake caught some orange tinted clouds as they drifted eastward over Marvel Pass and reflected the scene back up to the heavens. We crossed a talus fan on the southern shore and sat on some limestone boulders to watch the surreal arena below.

Back at camp, we took our food sack over to a meadow some distance from the tent and hung it from a large dead snag. It swung four metres above the ground and we wondered about the size of the bear that could swipe that offering down from its lofty mooring. We returned to our tent and built a fire in the stone firepit by the cabin, the only campfire I would enjoy all season. There is something about a campfire that captures the imagination. Its warmth and cheeriness beckons us back to the wild frontier when the fire was the hub of social activity, and further, back to our primitive ancestry, when all humankind lived in caves, foraging and enduring through countless seasons. We felt a quiet calmness come over us in that serene and delicate alpland.

~

My journal entry for the morning of July 26 reads: "It is seven am and I have just spent the most profoundly enjoyable hour of my hiking life so far. The early sun as it climbs skyward is lighting the peaks individually and defining their shapes with finely cast shadows."

This morning remains, as I write this, the most memorable one of the entire summer. Its simple loveliness and quiet beauty, and the crystal clarity of the air is still etched deeply in my memory. I scrambled from the confines of the tent as a pink blush painted the peaks above Aurora Creek. The cabin and tent were deep in morning shadows, but gradually the larch trees on the opposite shore started to receive the first warming rays of a new day. A later entry in the journal captures the moment: "I will remember this forever, and I am charged with emotion. The word stunning does not come close to describing the exquisite scene before me as I sit alone with my back against a larch tree. I feel pensive, peaceful, fulfilled and honoured that I could be here at this time."

Exactly one year ago to the day, I was sitting in the Tom Baker Cancer facility in Calgary with a needle in my wrist, receiving a life–prolonging chemical therapy treatment. If the Grim Reaper had crept up behind me as I worried away in that hospital chair, tapped me on the shoulder, winked and intoned, "Hang in there sonny, one year from today, you'll be up in heaven," The very last thing I would have thought of was Cabin Lake! But there I was, in a different kind of heaven, and oh so thankful to be there!

The reflections on the lake that morning were absolutely perfect; there wasn't a breath of wind. With only four exposures left in my camera, I had to be very selective in my photographic choices. Alex crawled out a bit later and we set about making breakfast and decamping. We found all sorts of reasons to avoid leaving our alpine utopia, and did not actually hoist our packs until past noon. As we topped out on the ridge behind camp, we stopped for one last look at the lake and meadowlands and thought about how Walter Wilcox and Bill Peyto must have felt as they traversed this plateau area in 1895, the first recorded passage of Marvel Pass by a white man. Wilcox had hired Peyto to take him by horse into Mount Assiniboine. He wanted to be the first man to climb the peak. In a reconnaissance trip that took them three days, they circumnavigated the base, and in so doing, became the first explorers to cross the uplands of the Marvel plateau.

At the top of the ridge, we came across a park boundary sign that was both perplexing and enlightening. The sign read "Entering Banff National Park," and a smaller sign on a nearby larch read "Marvel Pass." We dropped our packs and got the map out. Something here was obviously amiss. Our map very clearly showed the boundary, the Continental Divide, the border between Alberta and British Columbia, running through the Marvel plateau we had explored the day before. It also showed Cabin Lake to be well within the borders of Banff National Park. The night before, as we sat around the fire, I had casually wondered why, if the divide was west of our present position, was the water from Cabin Lake draining west, down to Aurora Creek, in B.C. Wasn't all water east of the divide supposed to drain east? Alex pondered that for a bit and suggested Marvel Pass was behind us, up on the ridge, which was in fact, true, though we had no way of knowing it at the time. I said that couldn't be, Cabin Lake was supposed to be in the park. We looked again at the map. Sure enough, the divide, according to the map, was west of us, the lake clearly shown inside the confines of Banff Park. Yet its waters drained west, and that was a plain fact!

Now here we were, apparently on the crest of the Continental Divide—if the sign was to be believed—about to enter Alberta and Banff National Park. If we chose to believe this was correct, we could now understand why Cabin Lake drained westward. It was because it was west of the divide! The boundary line drawn on the map was plainly wrong and Cabin Lake was definitely in B.C., not Alberta. It was interesting for me to note Alex's nonchalance with this glaring mistake. He said this stuff happens all the time, and as he had used maps extensively in his previous occupation as a park ranger, I guessed he was probably right. "Map's only as good as the guy who drew it," he said. I, on the other hand, had always believed maps to be absolutely correct in every minuscule detail.

Later on that summer, while doing research at Shadow Lake, I came across an interesting anecdote. Apparently, sometime in the 1950s, a trapper from B.C. secured a trapping permit from the B.C. Government, for an area around the headwaters of Aurora Creek. This self–reliant individual made his way up the drainages, coming from the west and eventually came to a small lake. It was here that he began felling trees and skidding them down to the lakeshore. Over the winter, with axe and saw, he started forming the walls of his cabin. One can only imagine the lonely work back there, the quiet cold, the darkness and remoteness.

Then one day, civil servants from our illustrious government came calling on him, and berated him for building a cabin in their national park. They would have shaken their heads and with an imperious gesture, pulled forth a survey map and jabbed frozen fingers along the line representing the provincial boundary, the Continental Divide. I can imagine the trapper's profane retort as his bearded chin and furrowed brow tried to come to grips with this ludicrous situation. "Hell–fire boys," He would have shouted. "Throw that damn map to the four winds! Why lookit the way the water flows fer crissakes, use your God–given brains!" But of course his rebuttals would fall on the deaf ears of the political machine, and his trapping rights would not be upheld by any court in the land. He left and that is why Alex and I never found any evidence of roof rafters or doors and windows; he had not been allowed to continue long enough to fashion these necessities. It was not until some years later that the mistake was noticed. The oversight was a blunder by a survey team back in the 1920s, working under Oliver Wheeler! Over the years, the maps that were produced used the information gleaned from his original survey notes.

For Alex and I, it was easy to understand how the error had occurred. To us, Marvel plateau had felt like a pass between two drainages, as I'm sure it did to the Wheeler surveyors. It was only when exploring the meadows that we noticed that lakelets on the escarpment to the east of our plateau were still draining west.

We put this interesting conundrum behind us and descended 400 metres to the damp meadows above Owl Lake. We hiked along and arrived at the lake in the heat of the afternoon. Owl was a large lake with an extensive gravel bar. Karst features and the exceedingly dry summer had allowed most of the water to drain away underground resulting in a gravel shoreline ringing the lake. We rested and ate some GORP here before dropping down into the Bryant Creek valley. En route, a cow moose with twin calves entertained us. We tried to get closer to them and with great stealth, we crept through the forest; but she had, of course got wind of us and they vanished like mosquitoes in a candle flame. By mid–afternoon, we had intersected the main Mount Shark trail. It follows the course of Bryant Creek as it rushed eastward to the Spray Lakes Reservoir. Within the hour, we were at Big Springs Campground and in this broad valley, with other tents and strangers about us, we felt our trip was over.

We had hiked about 13 kilometres that day, and still felt the wilderness tugging us back to Marvel Pass. We spent a long, warm sunny evening at Big Springs, eating whatever food we still had. The next day we would be heading out on the Mount Shark trail to reunite with our wives.

~

Hikers travelling this route will do well to divert to a natural feature in the area known as Karst Springs. We did, on our last morning out. The 20–minute side trip took us to the base of a limestone bluff. The water disgorges from under the bedrock with extreme turbulence and velocity. It is one of the largest springs of its kind in North America. The water is as clear and pure as it could possibly be, having just been filtered through 500 metres of limestone bedrock. The green, luxuriant mosses that live off this extremely cold water are vibrant and lush in the dark canopy of the surrounding forest. At the base of this rock is a clear pool, perhaps two metres deep and seven metres across. It was interesting to sit and speculate about where this large volume of water comes from. It seems probable that the water comes from some large lakes in high mountain basins which drain like sinks into the cavernous systems of the karst topography, running through the stony labyrinths deep within the bowels of the peaks.

The final push along the Mount Shark trail was tedious and frustrating. The trail was a roadbed now and was populated by every manner of outdoor enthusiast. Day hikers with howling babies, fluorescent joggers, horses and mountain bikers crowded the path, and every one of them seemed to be in a hurry. Some, I guess had only a few hours out here in which to enjoy the beauty, and understandably, they wanted to make the most of their time. Alex and I longed for the peace and quiet, the simple serenity of Aurora Creek.

For the remaining two kilometres, we also fit right in and made the most of our time, getting the hell out of there! Cecilia saw us smoking down the trail and was waiting at the truck with two frosty beers, fresh from the cooler, as we emerged in the hot dusty parking lot shortly after noon.

Boulder Hopping at Mistaya Lodge

The chattering noise of the incoming helicopter filled the valley. It swooped down into our position as we waited in a meadow on the banks of the Blaeberry River, about 30 kilometres from the town of Golden, B.C.

It was early morning on July 31 and Cecilia and I were on our way to a remote lodge high in an alpine basin at the headwaters of Wildcat Creek. Known as Mistaya Lodge it had been built in the early 1990s by Jane Girvan and Ron Blaue, two local entrepreneurs from the Golden area. It serves as a base for skiers in the winter as well as hikers and climbers during the summer months. The quiet location in the forest, near the tree line, is remote and very hard to hike into. While a trail does exist, the exceptionally steep nature of the path is such that few hardy souls attempt it. Virtually all the guests are transported to the lodge by Alpine Helicopters, a charter company based in Golden using a Bell 407 six–passenger helicopter.

As ground support staff loaded freight and food aboard the screaming machine, six of us clambered aboard and buckled in for the ten minute flight to the lodge. Once in the air, we set a course up the Blaeberry River drainage, flying over logging roads and past cutblocks. Even the commercial scars on the mountain flanks, land that was outside the protection of the nearby National Parks, could do little to diminish the beauty of the broad valley and the glaciers and snowfields that hung above it. The Mummery Glacier came into view over our left shoulder and within a few minutes, we banked to the northeast and climbed up Wildcat Creek. The chopper settled on the heli–pad on top of a rocky headwall, a short walk from the lodge. Jane was standing near the edge of the clearing, ready to escort her new charges down the gravelled path to the buildings.

Once inside, we were shown to our rooms, and then regrouped in the dining area for an informal talk given by Ron on matters regarding lodge etiquette and safety issues. The lodge is almost 2000 square feet and sits at an elevation of 2200 metres. We toured the premises and were shown the location of the two outhouses and the sauna building. There was also a tiny greenhouse, a tool shed and substantial staff quarters in the immediate area. Cecilia and I sat on the deck, looked out over the little pond in front of the lodge and watched humming birds dive bomb the feeder.

As one would expect, it is very peaceful up there. With only 14 guests staying at the lodge at any given time, there is adequate elbowroom; it would never feel crowded. I had spent the previous 30 days camping and was looking forward to a roof over my head, a comfortable bed and sumptuous dinner fare, while still being able to see some incredible mountain scenery in a remote setting.

That afternoon we joined a group of lodge guests on a familiarization tour of the basin. Jane came out onto the porch to lead the walk. She proved to be a very capable and confident person whose infectious enthusiasm endeared her guests to her almost immediately. While her knowledge of the local plants and flowers was nothing short of amazing, she also had a good understanding of the geology of the area. She pointed out various peaks and glaciers, saying she and Ron had named most of them. This remote basin had seldom been visited prior to their arrival in the late 1980s, hence the majority of the local features had been unnamed. After locating this high alpine valley on a topographic map, the two of them had explored this area and made plans to build a backcountry facility for skiers. Wildcat Basin is nestled in a nook between Banff and Yoho National Parks, lying just outside their boundaries. Its placement, right against the Continental Divide, ensures that it receives a great deal of moisture, snow in the winter months, and lots of rain in the summer. We were told as much as seven metres of snow falls here in a given winter, and the snow pack on the ground is usually three metres deep.

Later that day, as we viewed the panorama from Mohawk Ridge, it did indeed look like a basin, similar to the sink in your home, with the lodge and its bright red metal roof placed where the drain would be. Seven separate and distinct glaciers clung to the walls and rocky precipices that circled the basin in a 270–degree arc. Just below the lodge, Wildcat Creek cascades over the 70–metre headwall and charges down into the Blaeberry River valley, 14 kilometres away. This rocky headwall takes on the appearance of an impregnable fortress when viewed from below, and for this reason, few hikers climb up into the basin. In the wintertime, it was impossible to get snow machines past the headwall. Ron and Jane do not own this land, they lease it from the provincial government. However, because it is difficult for the general population to get up into valley, they enjoy a very private setting.

Back at the lodge in time for supper, we enjoyed a pre–dinner cocktail and met some of the guests at the dining table. We chatted with Barb and Richard Fearn, hikers we had met previously at Skoki Lodge. These friendly folks live in Florida, when they aren't out exploring the Canadian Rockies, an activity they had been devoted to over the last few years. They possessed a strong working knowledge of the various backcountry lodges and had an great appreciation for Canada's National Parks. It seemed they had stayed at every remote lodge we have here in the Canadian Rockies, at one time or another. The Fearns had taken the time to learn some of the geography and history of the Parks and appeared more enlightened than many of our fellow Canadians. We enjoyed their company very much. We spent the evening in quiet contentment, playing cards and visiting the lodge's substantial library.

~

During our visit to Mistaya Lodge the weather was quite changeable, as one would expect being so near the Continental Divide. The mornings would dawn bright and sunny, but soon clouds would move in over the divide, sometimes bringing rain. The temperature, while cool, was ideal for hiking and even if the sky was not always blue, the alpine flowers more than made up for the overcast days.

There are few established trails in the basin, so we wandered about wherever we wished. Cecilia and I enjoyed our time here together; we rarely came across other lodge guests while we were out, again because there were so few trails. While Ron and Jane had worked some trails into the scree slopes, the tundra grasses remained unmarked and hikers were advised to spread out, thus minimizing the damage done to the fragile alpine environment by hiking boots. The growing season up here is but a few short weeks and any damage done to the fragile vegetation could be permanent. Moss campion, for example, is a ground hugging plant, and flowers only once every 20 years in some harsh environments.

While we enjoyed roaming throughout the basin during our stay at the lodge, our favourite excursion was out to, what Ron and Jane had named Mista Vista. It is a vast rock outcropping in the upper basin, tucked in under Barbette and Mistaya mountains. These 3000–metre peaks form the backbone of the Continental Divide. In the valley to the east of these mountains, the Icefields Parkway winds through the Bow and Mistaya valleys on its way to Saskatchewan River Crossing.

Barbette is named for its resemblance to a ship. There are two large, flat limestone formations on this mountain, hence barbette, which, in naval parlance, is a rotating gun platform. Mistaya, is the Stoney Indian word for grizzly bear.

From the top of Mista Vista, we could see virtually everything the Wildcat Basin had to offer. Below our feet were three exquisite mountain tarns, Leprechaun, Longshadow and Stonebird. These lakes are fed by two small glaciers, Clamshell and Stonebird, both of which sit right on the Continental Divide. We visited these lakes during the long afternoon, rambling hither and yon, with no trail to follow, and spent a great deal of time admiring the stupendous array of wildflowers that grew in profusion on the shores of these delightful ponds. Karst Creek drains these lakelets, and we stopped to investigate the Karst Hole along the way. The stream dropped 30 metres into a dark, limestone chimney system and then follows the underground bedrock for perhaps a kilometre before debouching into Wildcat Creek.

Back at the lodge, we enjoyed a sauna. The sauna room itself, sheathed in aromatic cedar, is perhaps three metres by three metres and heated with wood from the adjacent forest. The deck that led to the sauna room is four metres above the ground so that it can be easily accessed in the heavy snows of winter. Every detail it seemed, had been carefully thought out by our enterprising hosts, both for the enjoyment of their guests and practicality. As we looked around, it was interesting to realize that every single item, from windows and doors to rafters and roofing material had been flown in to this site by helicopter. Every item here served a vital purpose in the running of the lodge, and everything here worked efficiently. Ron had even harnessed the power of Wildcat Creek to generate some electricity, and mounted solar panels on the roof of one of the buildings.

After a fabulous dinner of lamb one evening, Jane and Ron treated their guests to a video of the area, showcasing its many attributes in winter and summer. This video had been shown at trade shows throughout North America, to generate interest in the area and to hopefully create some new business. Part of the video showed some dramatic footage of a 4–year old grizzly digging ground squirrels from their burrows directly in front of the lodge windows! This bear had an interesting history. Clipped to his ear was a yellow tag, the number 67. Jane knew the National Parks policy was to tag and relocate problem bears, so she phoned down to Lake Louise to advise them of the location of this particular bruin. Parks officials were happy to receive the update and were able to give the lodge a rundown on the bear's movements over the past few days.

The grizzly had initially been trapped at a campground in Lake Louise village and then relocated to an alpine area north of Bow Lake, 50 kilometres away, on July 24. The next day, it was sighted on the shores of Peyto Lake and on the afternoon of July 26, it was busy feeding on Jane's front step! Now, for it to get into the Wildcat Basin, it must have travelled over the morainal debris at the southwest end of Peyto Lake, climbed up onto the Waputik Icefield, crossed over the Continental Divide, and descended the Stonebird Glacier to the valley below. The route taken by this bear was verified two days later when Ron, travelling with clients on the Stonebird Glacier, crossed the distinctive ursine paw prints.

The icy route that the bear took to arrive at Wildcat was certainly not typical bear behaviour and we questioned the current policies of the National Parks. Their strategy involves capturing problem bears in a culvert trap and then relocating them by helicopter to a remote area, usually in the Park, hoping that they will not return to their previous home. It was easy for us to imagine the trauma and fright that the bear would experience. First the bear would be confined in a metal trap and visited by any number of park wardens, biologists and other researchers. It would then be tranquillized. Currently, the "trank" used by our parks' service is Telazol and contains the chemical compounds Tiletamamine, hydrochlorine and Zolazepam. Currently, Telazol provides the safest intrusion on the bears' complex internal chemistry, allowing the grizzly to "come out" of his sedation relatively unscathed. The bear would be then manoeuvred into a net and slung unceremoniously beneath the screaming blades of a helicopter.

Finally, parks personnel would drop their inert cargo in an alpine basin or meadow back in a remote area of the park. They would then wait in the "chopper" to make sure their charge had not suffered any serious, debilitating effects from the administered drugs before flying off.

It is logical to assume that when a bear is airlifted out of it's home range, it will be unloaded into another bear's territory. Once relocated bears have recovered from the immobilizing drugs, they will quickly realize they are in another bear's habitat. Bears never deal well with stress and right away, a relocated bear would have to address the "fight or flight" question. The bear's sex may determine how it will respond to its new home. A boar may stay and try to fight and become dominant in the new territory; a sow may choose to leave and find a new home elsewhere. Almost assuredly, any bear, regardless of age or sex, will contemplate returning to where it came from, to return to the perceived safety of the home range.

To many of us, it seems fundamentally wrong to uproot bears from their home region and expect them to adapt to a new area. When this occurs the bear will become agitated and aggressive, until it settles down in the new territory. This can result in a dangerous situation for transient hikers passing through the bear's new location. In the case of bear #67, after being relocated at Bow Lake, it immediately decided to leave. It must have sensed that it didn't belong and ventured off in search of a safer environment. Hence its uncharacteristic journey over icefields and glaciers in an attempt to find a new home.

Bear relocation remains an ongoing problem for Parks Canada officials. They are charged with guaranteeing the safety of the public and, at the same time, they are mandated to protect an endangered species. It appears there is no simple solution.

~

On the next day, we covered a different part of the basin, hiking up the prominent drainage of Wildcat Creek, and onto the toe of the Wildcat Glacier. We got close enough to reach out and touch the gravel–studded ice. As there are no trails in the area, boulder hopping through the moraines is the only way to move beneath the ice and glaciers that cling to the cirques above. The Wildcat Glacier is the largest piece of ice in the vicinity, however several other minor hanging glaciers with names such as Nexus, Grindl and Boomerang, kept us entertained as we wound over to Mohawk Ridge that rainy afternoon. From the top of the ridge, we could look down 1000 metres, along Wildcat Creek to the distant valley of the Blaeberry River.

We could also see Doubt Hill, a local historic feature. It is located near Howse Pass and is where David Thompson wintered in 1803. Thompson was exploring a route to the Pacific Ocean and had been caught by the early snows of winter. His Indian guides had brought him over Howse Pass from the east to this location and knew the valley would eventually lead him and his party to the Columbia River. Thompson's men "doubted" the route would lead to the ocean, hence the name, Doubt Hill.

~

August 3 was our last morning at Mistaya Lodge. That morning the sun sparkled off the tarn in front of the lodge. We photographed the incredible reflections generated by the sun on the snow and icefields of the surrounding peaks as we waited for the helicopter to come up the valley and ferry us down to civilization, 20 minutes away.

Cecilia and I were the last passengers to be flown out, and so we had an extra hour in this forested utopia. The last shuttle came in and we were whisked off the face of the headwall, dropping with dizzying speed to the valley below. The pilot was a talkative sort and made the flight more interesting by pointing out local features, such as the Amiskiwi Pass and a couple of high–elevation tarns, set back in tiny cirques and almost assuredly never visited by humans. I was riding shotgun (the seat beside the pilot) and the views out the front of the Plexiglas bubble were so fantastic, I dared not blink! It was, for him, just another day in the office.

The nice thing about *his* job however was that the paintings on his office walls were always changing! We got a brief view of the icy splendour of the Freshfield group of mountains out to the northwest and another impressive look at the Mummery Glacier in the morning sunlight. Far too soon we were down in the Columbia River valley, clattering over the pastureland and on toward the airport at Golden. Our brief holiday was over, and I was left with an interesting thought. "Maybe I shouldn't have thought of being a park warden after all, maybe what I really should have been was a chopper pilot. Yeah, that's the life for me!"

To The Rockies Highest

The familiar sound of rain pattering down on the blue tarp filled my ears as Cecilia prepared dinner in the Lucerne campground near Mount Robson on the evening of August 3rd. Out on the highway, the traffic swished by, leaving long, misty wakes of airborne moisture behind. The camp attendant clomped over in his rubber boots and rain slicker to collect the $12 camping fee. He was a chatty kind of guy and when we mentioned to him that we were heading in to Berg Lake he said, "Yeah, been in there a few times. Really nice back there, lots of people, though." We asked him about the weather. "S'posed to be getting better. Heard a forecast this afternoon, but you never know around here. You guys got reservations?" We shook our heads. "Yeah, well good luck then! Long weekend and all, you may have to hang around a couple of days until a spot opens." We thought this might happen, but with the poor weather we hoped to sneak in on a cancellation. We went to bed in the back of the truck, cold and damp and wondering if we were going hiking the next day.

~

The following morning was foggy and threatening to rain. The mountains were hidden by valley cloud. We drove into the Visitor Centre at Mount Robson Provincial Park, and took our turn in line at the reservation desk. With an elevation gain of 800 metres over a distance of 25 kilometres, this trail, according to the printed literature was the most popular backpacking trail in the Canadian Rockies. I was not mollified. "Man oh man, standing in line just to hike in the woods," I thought to myself. "What's the world coming to?"

Mount Robson Provincial Park lies just over the Continental Divide in British Columbia, about 80 kilometres west of Jasper, Alberta. To protect both the environment and the highest peak in the Canadian Rockies, 2170 square kilometres was set aside by the provincial government in 1913. The British explorer Walter Cheadle was the first to describe the beauty of the mountain when he was guided through the region in 1863. "The upper portion dimmed by a necklace of light feathery clouds, beyond which its pointed apex of ice, glittering in the morning sun, shot up far into the blue heaven above." Cheadle did not need to stand in line to see Mount Robson and I chafed at having to do so now.

We intended to spend our first night at the Whitehorn campground, 11 kilometres along the trail to Berg Lake. The two people ahead of us in line were from Germany and, like us, did not have reservations, however they were able to secure the last tent site at the Whitehorn campground. However, we were not turned away as there were camping spots available at Kinney, Emperor and Berg. We paid $60 for six nights, two at Kinney Lake and four at Berg Lake and drove over to the trailhead. Cecilia cooked up lunch while I worked on our backpacks. We set out on the trail at noon, just as the clouds opened up and the rain started pelting down. Once in the woods, we immediately noticed the lush growth in the hemlock and red cedar forest. Some of the trees were over a metre in diameter and the forest floor was covered with beautiful ferns, devil's club, dogwood and thimbleberry.

I began to understand that the rain was an integral part of this forest environment. It is a moist pacific climate here; the hulking monolith of the Robson massif is a powerful influence. It generates a wonderfully fertile atmosphere. The rich odours of moss and cedar enveloped us as we climbed the trail to Kinney Lake. The campground is only seven kilometres from the trailhead and a suitable destination for a wild plethora of sightseers and day trippers. Even on this rainy day, the trail was crowded with hikers. Mount Robson is well known around the world and is a recognized Canadian hiking mecca for people from other countries. The attendant at the campground was right, there were lots of people on the trail and as it turned out, we were shoulder to shoulder with fellow hikers for the entire week. We always had to work hard to find quiet spaces for ourselves.

In 1907, Arthur P. Coleman, a glaciologist, along with his brother Quincy, and Reverend George B. Kinney, were the first Europeans to ascend the valley along the Robson River and discover a lake, which they later named Kinney Lake. They had come to the valley in an attempt to conquer Mount Robson, but were defeated both by the lateness of the season and a diminishing food supply.

When we reached Kinney Lake campground it was raining steadily and so we stood in the picnic shelter, waiting for a respite, sharing the small area with about 20 other damp hikers. We felt little camaraderie here and most groups kept to themselves, language barriers making casual banter impossible. While Cecilia got the pots out for dinner, I set the tent up in the wet forest and came back to a bowl of hot soup. Toward late evening, the skies cleared and afforded us our first glimpse of the summit ridge on Mount Robson. At 12,972 feet it was an astounding 10,000 feet above our heads! We were cautiously optimistic that the next day would bring fine weather in which to enjoy the splendour of Berg Lake. We rested that night in our tent and listened to the muted roar of a distant waterfall.

~

A morning wash in the blue–green waters of glacially fed Kinney Lake spurred us into a flurry of activity. We were both eager to get on the trail; the sun was shining and the day promised to be fine. I was excited. Today I would finally see Berg Lake, a mountain treasure that I had wanted to see all my life. Cecilia still retained a foggy memory of having visited the lake before, almost 40 years ago.

We began our hike along the raging Robson River as it hurtled along on it's way to an appointment with the distant Fraser River. Before long, we were ascending to the Valley of a Thousand Falls. On the way, the trail skirted and wound its way through a fairly recent rock avalanche. Huge boulders the size of pianos, half–tons and cabins, had crashed down on the forest and trail within the last few years. Large fir and spruce trees, their trunks snapped and shattered, remained as graphic evidence of the explosive nature of the slide; how incredible to have been on the trail at that time!

As we walked through the surreal landscape, we noted that rock avalanches had happened at other times; some of the large, garage–size boulders were covered with lichen and moss, some even supporting young trees, while the newest arrivals were clean and bright, as if they had just been cleaved from the face above.

We took a 30–minute rest at the Whitehorn campground, near the Robson River in the Valley of a Thousand Falls. It is a scenic area and much more appealing than Kinney Lake as a camping spot. There was a ranger cabin on the opposite bank of the river and high up on the rocky buttress above the cabin, a finger of the glacier on Mount Whitehorn poked over the lip towards the valley.

It had been a easy hike up to this point, but things were about to become serious, as in the next four kilometres we would ascend to the basin that held Berg Lake, 460 metres higher! We adjusted our packs, made sure we had enough water, and turned our bodies and thoughts to the gruelling climb ahead.

It was a long but rewarding trek up from below, with the Robson River a steady presence and the scenery changing around every bend in the trail. We passed three very dramatic cascades along the way, the most notable being Emperor Falls. We dropped our packs and approached the falls for a closer look at the massive display of raw power as water exploded through a rocky chasm in a trailside cliff band. The spray generated by the falls drifted over us and soaked us instantly. You could not hear anything above the incredible roar, and the noise and the freezing spray seemed to suck the air from our lungs. We stayed and shivered but a few moments before returning to the main trail.

The trail led us up a steep headwall to the basin holding Berg Lake and we got our first tantalizing view of the Mist Glacier as it dropped from the north face of Robson. The peak was wreathed in afternoon cloud, which to us was no surprise; the weather was unstable and there were showers about. We hoped, however, to see the top of Mount Robson sometime during our stay; we certainly had lots of time. The final push along the shore of Berg Lake was in abnormally windy conditions and we noted whitecaps on its surface. We arrived at the Hargreaves Shelter on the northeast side in the late afternoon, nonplussed by the number of hikers about, but pleased to be finally, at the lake. The Berg Lake campground was, apparently, the most popular on the trail and it seemed every camping spot had been spoken for. We rooted about and eventually found a site uphill, behind the shelter. Even though it was not the perfect spot, we felt it would have to do.

A cacophony of smells and noises greeted us as we entered the Hargreaves Shelter for dinner that evening. Originally built in 1927, it had been used by the Canadian National Railway, which brought tourists through the area by packtrain. It was subsequently sold to private interests in 1959, and in 1979, the Provincial Parks took it over and turned it into a backpacker's shelter; a much–appreciated facility during inclement weather. As it was presently raining, almost all the hikers in camp had decided to cook indoors. The heavy log walls and small windows created a dim and murky environment; the sounds of white gas, propane and butane stoves hissing on the tables, the smells and textures of various foods being prepared, the chattering of foreign tongues and the smell of sweat–stained clothing produced a rather odorous atmosphere. The experience was just the opposite to the solitude we were seeking; still, it was better than cooking outside with the wind and rain.

There were food storage lockers inside the shelter which was a comfort. We did not have to go and find a bear–hang, or wrap our food in plastic to protect it from the dampness. Amidst this noisy confusion, we bolted our food in the half–light, washed our dishes, stored our supplies, and vacated with haste to the relative peace in our tent. We had intended to stay up awhile, but with the present weather conditions, we thought it would be more of an enduring, rather than an endearing experience. So we tucked in early and rested our feet, which had pounded 14 kilometres of trail that day, caught up on our journals and read our books.

~

There is a host of trails in the immediate vicinity of Berg Lake. Snowbird Pass and Mumm Basin are two of the more appealing ones, but that first day at Berg Lake the weather was not very cooperative and so we opted for a visit to Adolphus Lake, a small mountain gem to the east of Robson Pass, in Jasper National Park. Except for the turbulent noise of a shuttle helicopter bringing in a volunteer trail crew from the Sierra Club, we had the environs of the pass to ourselves. In the space of five kilometres, we noticed a Park rangers cabin, two campgrounds, and a horse outfitters camp. Adolphus Lake sits just inside Alberta and was named by

Arthur P. Coleman in 1908 to honour his Indian guide, Adolphus Moberly. Coleman also named Berg Lake, for obvious reasons, and he called the icefall feeding the lake, the Blue Glacier. The pass itself is broad and flat and at a relatively low elevation of 1650 metres, hardly even discernible as a height of land between two drainages, let alone the apex of the Continental Divide.

In the early afternoon, we wandered over to the toe of the Robson Glacier to scout out the trail to Snowbird Pass. It seemed to be a demanding route with a lot of elevation gain, but given fair weather, it would be incredibly scenic. From the rocks above the marginal lake at the toe of the glacier, we could see the peaks and features I had read about in Conrad Kain's book, *Where the Clouds Can Go*. Kain led the first successful climb of Mount Robson in 1913, and described features such as the Extinguisher Tower, so named because it resembled a candle–snuffing device.

Looking back up toward Snowbird Pass, we noticed showery weather starting to descend into our valley and so we made our way back in increasing wind to the relative safety of the trees by the lakeshore. Later at the campground we managed to find a more acceptable tent site and we proceeded with the "Alex Shuffle," an operation, mentioned earlier, where you pick up your tent and parade through camp. Fortunately, nobody took notice as they had at Lake Magog, and no one had a laugh at our expense!

The vegetation at Berg Lake is very different from what we are used to in the eastern ranges of the Rockies. We had ascended 900 metres from the Yellowhead highway, and it certainly felt as if we were in the sub–alpine. If we had climbed this elevation above the Trans Canada highway at say, Lake Louise, we would be well above the tree line, probably in summit snowfields but here, at Berg Lake, we were still in deep forest. There were well–formed willow trees about as well as substantial stands of fir and spruce, generations old.

It was another cool, breezy evening. The shelter was stuffy and dark, and its lugubrious nature sent us running for the sanctuary of the tent shortly after we had cleaned up from dinner. It was still the best place to be. We wandered along the lakeshore in the gathering dusk and with Mount Robson still hidden by a heavy cloudbank, we said goodbye to the day. In our tent we read and listened to nearby Toboggan Falls as it rushed down into the lake from the high steppes of the Mumm basin.

~

The day we hiked up into the Mumm Basin, on the northern slopes above Berg Lake, remains one of the most rewarding days of the entire summer; the views were astonishing and the weather, magnificent. Arnold Mumm was a mountaineer who climbed in this region. His family, vintners by trade, were producers of the famous Mumm's champagne.

On this, our last day before heading out, we wanted to visit the Mumm Basin, even though the weather was marginal. As we climbed the 400 metres, the clouds burned off and we were the recipients of the most remarkable scenery. To see the blue sky and dazzling sun after so many days of cloud was like a shot of adrenaline, and we scurried up to the alpine meadows, redolent with the dancing rays of sunlight. We had waited four days to be treated, at long last, to a breathtaking view of the corniced summit snows on Mount Robson. It was in the high meadows of the Mumm Basin that we spent seven hours in the alpine, meandering wherever we wished, always within sight of the summit of Mount Robson. We were now at an elevation of over 2300 metres, and 1300 metres above our truck, yet still almost 2000 metres below Robson's icy summit.

We would not let this day end; we willed the gorgeous sun to stop in the sky, and could almost feel the mountains talking with us. While there were a few other hikers about, we were exploring off trail and were able to stay away from them, which allowed for a more unique and quiet experience. There was a large colony of hoary marmots on the ridge and it seemed each one had its own granite boulder to sit on, snooze and marvel at the unfolding splendour of the day. At one point, from where we sat, we could see five different marmots on five different limestone boulders; it was as if they were appreciating the returning warmth of the sun, just as we were.

Berg Lake, 400 metres below trapped the passing cloud shadows as they drifted across the turquoise surface of the lake. Even at this height, we could see small icebergs floating on the tranquil surface, little "bergy bits" that had calved from the Berg Glacier. The day was advancing, but we were reluctant to head down; we would walk a few paces, then drop to our butts, just to enjoy the simple magnificence of viewing the very highest mountain in all the Canadian Rockies!

We sat upon sun-warmed grasses in a tiny amphitheatre of rocks overlooking the lake and thought back to earlier times; how incredibly impressive this area must have appeared to the first adventurers! Coleman, in 1907 and 1908, and the Reverend Kinney, trying over three successive years to scale the icy monolith framed in perpetual ice and snow. With Donald Phillips, Kinney almost realized his dream in 1909, when the two of them came within a few metres of the summit. The peak was finally climbed in 1913, when William Foster and Albert MacCarthy stood on the snows of the summit with their guide, the redoubtable Conrad Kain. Foster, with simple eloquence, later wrote, "A panorama was unfolded that can never be described. Two thousand feet higher than any other mountain, as though at the masthead, we beheld a sea of mountains, glaciers, snowfields, lakes and waterways displayed in an endless array."

The mesmerizing scenic splendour of this grand peak will live in our hearts forever. As the sun dropped from its zenith, and began its long, sweeping arc to the west, we reluctantly pointed our boots downhill. It was now evening and the lower forests were draped in dusty shadows of grey and green.

The trail descends along the banks of Toboggan Creek, which races over the underlying bedrock, the exposed strata breaking its rush as it angles across the water flow. The result is a very noisy watercourse as the trapped water, pulled by gravity, hurtles down to Berg Lake, far below. It is an intensely fast moving stream sluicing across the bedrock, splashing in and out of small catch basins; a moving mass of foaming white. We continued to descend through the sultry light of evening.

Back at camp, we chatted over dinner with a family from North Dakota who had gone up to Snowbird Pass that day, marvelling at the extensive Reef Glacier visible to them from the summit. We in turn painted a wonderful picture of our experiences up in the Mumm Basin.

Cecilia and I headed to our tent as darkness settled into the valley. As I was waiting for her to get comfortable in the tent, I glanced through the forest at the upper slopes of Robson, bathed in the unearthly orange of an alpenglow. An alpenglow is a blush that comes upon the upper icefields of the mountains just before dark. An orange light is refracted off the clouds from the extremely low angle of the sun after it has set. It does not happen often and is always a treat to see, similar perhaps to experiencing the northern lights. "Cecilia, come quick!" I yelled into the tent, "You just have to see this!" She came smoking out of the tent like there was a snake in there and, grabbing the camera, we shuffled down to the lakeshore in unlaced boots to take in the dramatic evening twilight on the glaciated summit. We were not alone; several of us stood in quiet reverence to watch nature dance with fire. It was inspiring to watch our fellow tent mates, from distant countries, different environments and varying ages all drawn together in humble acquiescence to a greater spirit. The surreal light was over in an instant, fading from brilliant tangerine to a soft beige in a heartbeat, and we trundled off to our tents with smiles on our happy faces. Another memory yet so much more.

~

It was 5:30 am and I lay on my back in the tent, quietly watching the grey light steal through the nylon walls. "I really should get up. Just in case it's clear." I thought quietly to myself. It had clouded over the previous evening and I had no reason to suspect a clear dawn, however, it was our last morning at the lake. "I really should make the effort." I unwillingly exited my warm cocoon and sleepily peered about. A–crystal clear mountain dawn was unfolding before my very eyes! I dived back inside for my Canon camera, and hurriedly informed my sleeping spouse of the magic happening at her tent door. Then I was off, down to the lake to be the first to see the incredible dawn. It appeared that I was the only one moving about and I scampered around, like some demented, bow–legged leprechaun, chortling and cackling away to myself; the treasure was mine, all mine! I fastened my eyes on the unfolding drama. I searched about for different camera angles as the sun sparkled and danced on the crystallized snows of the Robson massif.

The sky was clear, not a cloud in sight, and the sun was just starting to dust Robson's lower icefields. It took another 30 minutes for the sun to spread its charm on the flat plane of the lake. The top of Mount Robson was an exquisite mass of white snow and ice, while the sky behind was the deepest indigo. Cecilia met me by the lake and quietly took my hand and we watched the sun caress the lower slopes and ridges of this special mountain; it looked like the stairway to heaven. The Shuswap, who had travelled through there for untold centuries referred to the mountain as Yuh–hai–has–kun, the "mountain of the spiral road."

The camp gradually came to life, and as we cooked our porridge on the front porch, in sight of the lake and peak, it was fun to hear the exclamations of glee and delight from the awakening hikers as they weaved their sleepy way to the lakeshore. We ate our breakfast to the music of clicking cameras, then caught up on our journals and sat, enchanted by the unfolding panorama about us. We struck camp by mid–morning for the 20 kilometre trip down to our truck. Our snail–like pace ensured that we would not get out before dark but little did we care as the brilliance of the day swept us along with awesome views in all directions.

Especially enjoyable was the striking view of Mount Whitehorn, which had been fully hidden by clouds on the trip into Berg Lake. The peak is horn shaped and draped in perpetual snow and ice. It was first climbed on August 10, 1911, by Conrad Kain, who made a fantastic solo ascent over the ice and rocks to the corniced summit. A. O. Wheeler was doing survey work in the area for the Boundary Commission at the time and Kain was acting as a guide to the surveyors as they ascended various peaks in order to take their transit readings. Kain, a normally very optimistic man, later wrote in his book, "I had absolutely no pleasure on that climb, the time was too short and the dangers too great."

The day was moving along, yet we were in no hurry to vacate this alpine basin. We had reserved a campsite at Kinney Lake for the night if we found the day was too long for us. We crossed the alluvial outwash of Hargreaves Creek, waved good–bye to the Berg and Mist glaciers, and all too soon dropped off the edge of the highland and into the Robson River valley.

Within three hours we arrived at the Whitehorn Campground, an elevation drop of 400 metres in nine kilometres. Immediately we were inundated with a wide variety of day trippers up from the valley bottom. While most of them seemed to belong, some hikers stood out. There were teenagers wearing light sneakers, T–shirts and halter tops and little else, with no apparent food or day packs. A couple of ladies strolled along in casual slacks, coiffed hair and earrings, sweaters casually draped over a forearm as if they were parading through the venerated halls of the Chateau Lake Louise; and there was one gentleman, in light shoes and a long–sleeved shirt carrying some sort of satchel like briefcase. All these people had made it in here—a distance of over ten kilometres under their own steam; they certainly had more fortitude than I would have given them credit for.

I do not believe I could have walked ten kilometres if I had possessed some of their footwear, and what if the weather turned? Running shoes on a slippery, muddy trail? What about a rain jacket and some extra food? Sometimes God looks after these hapless souls, sometimes not and the park rangers are called in to initiate a search and rescue operation.

After a short rest and some people–watching we continued our descent to Kinney Lake, stepping aside at one point to let a couple go by. They were on a steep section of trail, and applying themselves to the arduous task at hand; they were carrying a large cooler between them! At Kinney Lake, we heated up some soup and dumplings in the warm afternoon sun. It was just 5:30 pm and we knew we could make it down to the truck before dark, it being only another seven kilometres away.

We arrived at the truck shortly after the sun dipped below Mount Whitehorn, tired, smelly and hungry. The first order of business was to get into the Robson Campground on the highway, secure a tent site and head to the showers. As we drove through the camp, looking for a spot, our truck seemed to come to a stop on it's own smack in front of the shower house! We piled out, grabbed our towels and soap, left the truck parked illegally in front of the woodpile, and raced to the washhouse, clean clothes under our arms. Forty–five minutes later, two entirely new individuals emerged from the steamy interior.

Once in the truck we looked at each other quizzically, was our imagination playing tricks on us, or could we *really* smell Kentucky Fried Chicken wafting across the miles from Jasper Town? We believed we could smell that chicken and hastily set off in the truck, first stopping at the Camp Manager's trailer with an offer to pay for the showers. When she heard of our odorous condition on our return from Berg Lake, she understood the reason for the quick shower; when I explained that we could not linger because we were sure we could smell the KFC in Jasper, she just laughed out loud and waved us on our way, "I know what it's like when you come out of the woods. Drive safe you guys. Remember, KFC closes at ten o'clock and its 80 klicks away!"

Now the pressure was really on and we beat a hasty track eastward as the sun sank into the western horizon behind the truck. It was turning into a very long day. If I had possessed a riding crop, I would have used it on the truck door as we careened along, hunched over the steering wheel, hell bent to keep a rendezvous with a chicken in Jasper. I was kept busy trying to keep the shiny side up and the greasy side down on my half–ton. Between Mount Robson Provincial Park and Jasper town there is but one traffic light; we hit it red! It seemed to me that we smoked into town on two wheels, slammed the truck into a curbside space and hit the door to KFC at 10:03. We were met by vacant stares from the two kids inside, eye rolling looks that told us we were late, waaaay too late dude. "We are like, so closed!" Their body language spoke volumes. I wanted to pound on the doors and appeal to their sense of decency and justice! "C'mon you guys, we've just come down from Berg Lake, and we are really starved." But I had a feeling I knew what their response might be. "Ah berglake dude, whatsa berglake? Zat some kinda frozen slush man?"

RAMPARTS OF THE TONQUIN

In the warm sunshine of a new day, I meandered along the main street in Jasper. I was on my way back to the laundromat, when I spotted my hiking partner taking her ease on a bench in the town park. As she raised her eyebrows, I smiled and shook my head, "It's way too much, dear. It's going to cost at least 60 dollars." We were in the midst of getting things in order for our next backcountry trip, this one to the Amethyst Lakes, southwest of Jasper. We were puzzling over where we should park the truck, because there are two different trailheads for the hike.

The 50 kilometre hike in and out of the Tonquin Valley takes the form of a horseshoe, starting at the Astoria River on the road to Mount Edith Cavell, and finishing at Portal Creek, on the road to the Marmot Basin ski hill. How to get back to our truck at the Edith Cavell trailhead was causing a bit of a concern for us. There was a local taxi company that transferred hikers between these two points on a regular basis, and they had suggested we drive our truck to the Portal Creek trailhead and wait for them to meet us there. Then, they would shuttle us over to the Youth Hostel on the Edith Cavell road which is near the Astoria River trailhead, a distance of about 23 kilometres. The charge for this however, was just too much for our tight budget, so we decided that we would have to try and hitch a ride with some friendly soul upon our egress from Portal Creek. We didn't like our chances; as a general rule of thumb, a ski hill road doesn't see a lot of traffic during a hot summer day in August.

~

We left Jasper early the following day and drove up the winding road to the Astoria River trailhead. On that sultry, cloudless summer morning we shouldered our packs and struck off on the 17–kilometre climb to the high valley that holds the Amethyst Lakes. Our first stop was for lunch on the banks of the turbulent Verdant Creek, five kilometres along the trail. The stream drains from two picturesque, high–country lakes, Beryl and Buttress. Because there is no recognized trail to the turquoise gems, a hiker would be assured of having a peaceful experience in pristine beauty in those remote cirques.

After lunch we hiked beside the Astoria River for a few kilometres before beginning the torturous ascent into the Tonquin Valley. In the next valley to the south of us lay the richly historic Athabasca Pass, a route used extensively by fur traders during the last century. The pass, discovered by David Thompson in 1811, was the route favoured by the fur brigades until around 1850. In our valley, the Astoria River we were hiking beside, was named for a fur trading post at the mouth of the Columbia River on the West Coast. The name Tonquin was derived from an ocean going trading vessel used by John Jacob Astor, the fur trade magnate.

As we climbed out of the valley in the searing heat of the afternoon, we missed the friendly, cooling presence of the Astoria. There were about 20 switchbacks to negotiate as we climbed the 400 metres to the sub–alpine meadows. As we churned up the lower slopes of Oldhorn Mountain, we stopped and stepped to the side as a couple of wranglers and three horses came down the trail. After "howdys," they asked us if we had seen a horse go by. Earlier in the day, apparently, this horse had snapped his halter shank, snorted and thundered off down the trail. We shook our heads, we hadn't seen a horse anywhere around. They eased on by, and the cowboy who was riding sweep leaned over to me and drawled, "Ya sure you didn't see no horse?" I kind of squinted up at him, sitting there in the saddle, and thought, now what kind of question was that? "Well, ya know, I think we'd a probably noticed something that big crashing down the trail on top of us," I sarcastically replied. "Well, we're short one pony, that's fer sure, I don't know where the hell that crazy bronc run off to." I almost had the feeling he wanted to check our packs. Maybe we weren't hikers after all, no siree, maybe we were low down horse thieves with backpacks!

Toward late afternoon, we entered the meadows under Mount Clitheroe and caught our first glimpse of the Ramparts through the forested slopes ahead. They were spectacular. The views about us opened up; we could look back down the valley to distant Edith Cavell and across at Throne Mountain, so named for its likeness to a giant armchair. To the southwest, we could see into the Eremite Valley and Chrome Lake, shimmering in the late afternoon sun; aptly named, I thought. We pulled into the Switchback campground—our home for the night—and dropped our sweat–stained packs to the ground. We were the only campers there and we were given a feisty reception by the resident mosquito population. I think perhaps we must have been the first fresh blood they had seen in several days and these nefarious nightmares from hell almost bowled us over in their hurry to feast upon our tired bodies. They were just outrageous and we scrambled to find our head nets and gloves before doing anything else.

As we searched through the campsite, we realized there was no water close by; also, the tenting area was down, off the trail in a thick grove of trees, effectively shutting off any views and any breeze. We were pretty tired, having hiked 14 kilometres, so we sat on the ground, ate some GORP and chocolate and tried to find some energy.

"There's gotta be some water around here somewhere. How the hell can you build a campground and have no water?" I was hot, frustrated and tired. We scouted around a bit more and finally found a small seep in the moss. Because of the hot, dry summer that year combined with the lack of snow over the previous winter, the seep had virtually dried up. "Can't stay here honey, not without water. Maybe we should go on to Clitheroe, its only another three kilometres," I suggested. I knew Cecilia had had enough of her day and I was reluctant to ask her to continue. But slowly we resigned ourselves to moving along, so we heaved our packs up off the ground and slowly plodded back out to the main trail. It was the right decision; we just hoped there would be lots of water at the next campground. We wanted to, if possible have a good wash in camp. We were soaking with sweat from the day's exertions, it was closing in on seven pm and the temperature was still 28°C.

We watched for water as we trudged over to Clitheroe in the evening twilight, but found none and we began to wonder just how far would we have to go to slake our parched throats. Usually, we carry enough water with us, but on our hot, dusty ascent up the trail that afternoon, we had drained every drop of our reserve, thinking we would get some fresh water on our arrival at Switchback.

We found Clitheroe Campground and dropped our packs on the first available tent site. While there was a marginal seep close by, one would have a hard time calling it a stream. There was one other tent here, and the occupants waved at us from behind their protective screen nets. Unfortunately, the mosquitoes were here as well. We both washed and as Cecilia scrambled for the foodsack and dinner utensils, I hastily erected our tent against the overwhelming horde of winged warriors. We bolted our meagre dinner and jumped into our nylon nirvana. Where would we be without the comfort and safety of the tent? How would it be possible to manage the mosquitoes and deer flies? The combination of our body heat and blood had them swarming on the netting of the tent and brought back the stark terror of Baker Lake. There were also horseflies about, probably here as a result of the equestrian traffic that passed through the area. Our feet were tired from the 17–kilometre day and we went peacefully to sleep with thoughts of exploring the gorgeous area in the days ahead.

~

A grand and glorious day was about to unfold as I thrashed through the waist–high willow bushes a few hundred metres from camp, looking for that perfect spot to set up my tripod. I had, gratefully, come across a lovely, clear stream about five minutes from camp, the first real water I had encountered since leaving the Astoria River the day before. From its banks I watched the early morning sun play along the ridges and craggy precipices collectively known as the Ramparts. Resting on the lower slopes of Mount Clitheroe, I had my first, all encompassing view of this formidable chain of peaks, 12 separate mountains forming what appears to be an impressive line of defence on the Continental Divide. They are spread out over a distance of 14 kilometres above the Tonquin Valley, and many of the cliff faces soar fully a 1000 metres above the surface of the Amethyst Lakes.

In the chill of dawn, the flies had not yet risen from the grasses to begin their daily assault and I was content to just sit and let the morning sing to my senses. Looking out over the lakes from this vantage point on the lower slopes of the mountain, I was reminded of a picture I have in my library at home, a picture of Byron Harmon resting in these meadows, his camera beside him on a tripod, the photo titled, "Waiting for the Light." That particular image was taken in 1918, shortly after the area had been recognized for its' unique and unspoiled climbing potential by A. O. Wheeler the president of the Alpine Club of Canada. Unlike Harmon, I did not have to wait for the proper light; I was able to snap photos at leisure and I took full measure of the pristine beauty.

The first European to see and photograph this area was a surveyor by the name of M. P. Bridgeland, who came to this high plateau by way of Marmot Pass. The year was 1915 and the images he generated stirred much interest in this gorgeous area of Jasper National Park. He wrote, "This valley with its beautifully coloured lakes, its wide meadows and park–like forests, and its majestic peaks, is one of the most beautiful spots in the mountains." In 1918 Byron Harmon took the first motion pictures of the Ramparts and later, in 1928, Ansel Adams visited the area. At that time, he was the Sierra Club's professional photographer. The scenic value of this unspoiled wilderness was being spread far and wide.

The Ramparts and the Amethyst Lakes were a mesmerizing tonic to my soul and I sat enthralled as the new light played over these beautiful mountains. As long as I could remember, this had been a place I had wanted to explore and I wondered idly why I had waited so long. In a sense, there was an answer, though it seemed somewhat illogical. The only hikers we had talked with on this trip were from Red Deer, Alberta, and while we were in at Mount Robson the week before, most of the people with whom we had conversed were from areas in central Alberta. I believed that many outdoor adventurers from central and northern Alberta focus on this part of the Rocky Mountains and the area around the town of Jasper for their recreational outings. By the same token, many hikers from southern Alberta are very familiar with the environs of Waterton Lakes National Park. I was raised in Calgary and naturally, in my younger years, I gravitated to the sights of Banff and Lake Louise. For me, it seemed a daunting task indeed to set a hiking goal farther afield on the Icefields Parkway, such as the

Tonquin Valley or Mount Robson. Why? Look at all the incredible scenery I would have to travel past just to get to the trailhead! There was just so much to appreciate and investigate in my own backyard, it seemed I could not pass by these local treasures, just to search for other jewels that were farther away.

I sat and listened and felt as Wheeler must have felt when he was guided in here for the first time. He wrote. "The south wall and its great icebound escarpments... the view was magnificent beyond conception. It is a scene whose memory a lifetime cannot efface." I ambled back down into the forest and set the coffee to boiling, hoping to entice Cecilia from her warm slumber. This was hard to accomplish, as the previous day had been tiring for us both, but gradually, the aroma of fresh brewed java laced with some rye and sambuca, coaxed her from her bed.

After a breakfast of porridge and hydrated strawberries, we left camp to hike over to Surprise Point campground. This spot was on the southern shore of the Amethyst Lakes and while it was very buggy, it was also incredibly scenic. Given a strong breeze to keep the bugs away, this would make a pleasing camping spot. We spent several hours rambling along the lakeshore; the views were breathtaking and the day was hot, clear and cloudless. However, we were starting to notice a smoky haze from distant forest fires beginning to infiltrate our alpine basin. A few years ago, Cecilia had painted a canvas of this lake from a photograph taken out of a book by George Brybycin; we walked the shore trying to find the precise location. I took a photograph along this shore that later became our Christmas card for 2001.

We returned across the soggy, boggy, bug–infested meadowland that fringed the lakeshore and stopped by the park patrol cabin. The warden and his wife had come in on horseback two days previously and were headed out the following morning. He was a seasonal warden and expressed surprise at the lack of hiker activity. Normally, he told us, the Tonquin was a heavily used area, but with the unusually hot weather and the awful mosquitoes he felt perhaps the hikers were waiting for more favourable conditions. He also advised us to stay alert and be careful with our food storage, as there was a grizzly with cubs in the area; he had seen fresh tracks in the meadow that morning. He went on to say that this particular bear was well–known to parks staff, and was in fact a local bear, born and raised in the Tonquin. The sow was between six and seven years old and was presently raising her second litter. She was regarded as a good bear, able to keep herself and her offspring away from the hundreds of hikers that came into her domain each year. Still, she was a sow with cubs and so, he suggested we certainly needed to keep a watchful eye.

~

The following morning was blue, hot and full of bugs, and our fellow hikers had already folded their tent in preparation for the trip out along the Astoria River. We were going in the other direction, along the lakeshore and over to MacCarib Creek. We waved our porridge–encrusted spoons at them as they tracked through the trees to the main trail. Shortly thereafter, the warden and his wife came through, astride their mounts. They too, were headed out by way of the Astoria, getting an early start they explained, as it was easier on the horses, what with the heat and flies. We were left on our own in the immensity of this mountain majesty, however we too packed up quickly; we were scared the mosquitoes might find out that we were the only two people left!

Hiking on a horse trail is never much fun, and this particular path was no exception. Initially laid down over glacial till and truck–sized boulders, the trail could be a quagmire of clay, mud and roots in which horses sunk to their cinches during wet weather. With the present dry conditions however, the trail was iron hard, but with a very uneven trail tread, and we had to be ever vigilant not to step into a hoof–created hole. In the early years, this area was primarily accessed by people on horseback and it is still, perhaps the best way to travel through the muskeg which is so prevalent here. As hikers, we felt this part of the park was still pretty much thought of as horse country, with little attention paid to trail maintenance. Horses and hikers do not mix. The ideal situation would be to have a trail parallel, or in close proximity to, the horse trail, for use by hikers only. At present, there are two horse outfitters camps on the shores of the Amethyst Lakes. While there is substantial grass and meadowland on which to graze the horses, such camps are an environmental concern as this area is also a critical summer food source for a resident herd of mountain caribou. Parks information suggests that the current herd is comprised of about 35 animals. While the administration in Jasper National Park is committed to maintaining adequate forage for this fragile caribou herd, they are also keenly aware of the fiscal gain to the park from revenues generated by these two outfitting ventures. These backcountry lodges also provide ski touring packages in the winter months. This activity has little or no detrimental effect on the caribou as their winter food is chiefly comprised of lichen and moss that grows on rocks, bushes and trees. It is the sedges and grasses of summer that they rely on and have to share with the horses.

We hiked across this rich pastureland and spied some whitewashed cabins nestled among the trees. Tonquin Valley Adventures, formally known as Amethyst Lake Pack Trips is a horse camp located near the peninsula separating the two lakes. We dropped our packs beside the trail and walked around the cabins, searching for someone who could give us some information on the operation, but there was no one about, and no horses in the corral. The guests and wranglers appeared to be out on a ride. There were several old but serviceable cabins dispersed throughout the immediate locale, along with a larger cabin evidently used as a sitting–reading room and a newer log structure that served as a kitchen–dining room. Down by the lake, amongst the cotton grass, several rowboats lay overturned on the shore. Sitting on a height of land, the operation provided outstanding views of the lakes and Ramparts opposite. It looked like the camp had been there for many years.

As we hiked the trail that skirted along the eastern shore of the Amethyst Lakes we came upon the camp cook, returning from her morning wash in the lake. Her spontaneous happiness was a joy to behold. We asked her about the camp and she told us it had been in operation since 1939. Originally built by Fred Brewster, it was sold in 1956 to one of the wranglers, Tom Vinson. Vinson's daughter and her husband have operated the lodge for the past 25–five years. The camp provides horse and hiking trips in the summer, and backcountry ski trips during the winter. People that work in backcountry lodges always seem so exuberant and full of life; their infectious enthusiasm appears to be boundless! Far from the crowds and stress of the cities, is it possible that these quiet mountains are all anyone really needs? Her obvious health and vitality spoke volumes about life out here.

We hiked a little farther on down the lakeshore before quartering away in a northeasterly direction toward the MacCarib Creek drainage. As we gained elevation above the lakes, a new aspect of the Ramparts presented itself; the dramatic northern precipices came into view above Tonquin Pass. We had not been in position to see these beautifully–formed castellated ridges before now. They captured our imagination and we feasted our eyes upon their stony countenance as we ascended through the forest that hot afternoon. These were the peaks that had inspired the artist, A. Y. Jackson. He created a classic painting entitled "The Ramparts," in 1924. With names like Bastion, Turret, Geike and Barbican, they complemented their neighbours to the south. Those peaks had names such as Drawbridge, Redoubt, Dungeon and Parapet. These names were applied by the Boundary Commission of 1916, and were apparently given to reflect the fortress– or castle–like nature of these seemingly impregnable walls. We could see the other horse outfitter camp, nestled in the shoreline forest at the base of these formidable crags.

MacCarib Creek flowed beside our tent at the campground that hot afternoon, and provided us with clear drinking water, a refreshing bath, and the soft, tinkling music of its water as it passed over the stream–side gravel. The campground itself sat on a sparsely treed bench above the creek, at an elevation of 2000 metres. The views afforded from the site were inspiring and included the sweeping span of the Ramparts in the west, while to the east one could look over the upper meadows along the route to MacCarib Pass and Chak Peak. The stream banks were hemmed in by Mount Clitheroe to the south and the rocky escarpment of the Trident Range to the north. We glassed the upper meadows and ridges during the afternoon, looking for the elusive caribou known to inhabit those slopes, but we were not rewarded for our efforts. The exposed nature of the campsite made me wonder how the place would fare during severe mountain weather, with strong wind and lightning. Gazing up into the azure blue, I knew we would not know the answer to that concern during this particular visit.

Later, toward evening, Cecilia and I went over to visit with Percy, who was resting comfortably 50 metres from our tent. He had in fact, been resting there for about 70 years! Percy Goodair was a park warden who died on MacCarib ridge in 1929. A well–preserved stone marker lies above his final resting place. There used to be a patrol cabin here, in the 1920s, and Percy was found dead, near his porch, his body ravaged by a grizzly bear. With an axe nearby, it was surmised that he had been out chopping wood during a late September afternoon and been surprised by the bear. His official warden diary, found in his cabin, had notations in it pertaining to previous confrontations with a troublesome bear. He has the distinction of being the first National Park warden killed while on active duty. A mountain, directly behind the Ramparts was later named in his memory.

When we returned, we visited with two hikers, Trish and Marco. They had just come up the trail from Portal Creek campground where they had spent a sleepless night. There were now six of us in the camp, and these two recent arrivals had an interesting story to relate. We walked over to their tent as they regaled the other couple. Trish and Marco had pulled into the campground at Portal Creek, the previous afternoon about five pm. As they began to set up their camp, they turned to see a sow grizzly and cub watching them intently from the trail below. The bruins then ambled in an unhurried fashion down Portal Creek and out of sight, leaving behind two trembling trekkers. They couldn't go back to the safety of their car at the trailhead, because that was the way the bears had been headed. They couldn't continue on to the next camp as it was too late in the day. They were rational enough to understand that the sow was apparently simply curious, so they decided to sit tight. As there was nothing else they could do, they sat down to dinner. As it turned out, they were the only ones to enjoy the lonely ambience of the valley that evening; there were no other hikers in the vicinity.

Portal Creek campground was the location of a fatal bear mauling in 1992, an event of which these two hikers were well aware. That particular tragedy involved a similar couple, who surprised a grizzly bear upon entering the campsite to set up their tent. The girl climbed high into a tree, however her male companion was charged and killed. Officials were alerted by some other hikers who had run back down the trail to raise the alarm. Park wardens flew in by helicopter later that same evening and shot a grizzly, still in the campground. The eerie coincidence was not lost on Trish and Marco and consequently sleep did not pay them a visit that night. Here at MacCarib, they were happy to see two other tents, both for safety and company. We all enjoyed our individual dinners and the happy banter of the backcountry.

Thunderheads were building in the west, over the Ramparts and a shower swept through camp after dinner. It quickly passed and the region became suffused with the golden twilight of a lingering sun, the vibrant light sparkling in the soaking forest canopy. The Trident Range was lit in Day–Glo orange and black storm clouds played across the summit ridges.

The following morning, with a hot coffee in hand, I went over to talk to Marco, who was busy packing up his camp. As they were going over the same trails that Cecilia and I had just traversed, I was able to give him a bit of local knowledge on campsites, water availability and trail conditions. I asked him how they were going to get back to their car, as they were going out the Astoria River, and he said he had considered that problem; that was why they were doing the hike from Portal to the hostel. "The way I got it figured, there has to be lots of people up at the Youth Hostel, and I should be able to bum a ride down easily enough. Then all I have do is get up to Portal." I suggested to him that, if he felt comfortable with the idea, we could borrow his car keys. "Our truck's up at Astoria and we're going to have to hitch to get back there. We could take your car up the road, park it for you and hide the keys." He nodded his head. "Yeah, that's cool with me. Just take it easy though, eh." He grinned. "It's a new Jetta. Don't go smokin' up the tires!"

While I was engaged in negotiating a means of transportation, Cecilia was whomping up our morning meal and visiting with the other couple, Bev and Randy, from Kelowna. They were hiking out the Astoria River as well, in three days time. Because there was the two of us, they wondered if it would be possible for us to take their Jeep on up to the trailhead as well? It seemed we all shared the same concerns about hitching rides back to our respective autos.

As I took the tent down and secured it to my pack, I became lost in thought. Here in the backcountry, everything was distilled to simple basics. Yesterday, the camp cook's happy banter with strangers had seemed so natural. Today, people we had never met before were giving us the keys to their vehicles. These simple acts of honesty and trust have long been lost back in civilization. Hikers and wilderness wanderers will sometimes espouse on the reasons why they trek into the far valleys; to get in touch with themselves, with nature, with reality, they say. Cecilia and I felt rejuvenated in body and spirit; we treated nature with gentle hands back here and were rewarded with treasures beyond comprehension. Here, without a great leap of faith, we were able to believe in the basic honesty and intrinsic goodness of our fellow hikers. We, by definition, enjoyed a camaraderie with these like–minded souls, and knew that they were appreciating the same rewards for their efforts, as we were. Is the wilderness a tonic for the soul? Need you even ask?

The meadowland to the east, as it wound up to MacCarib Pass provided us with exceptional hiking during the morning. The creek that flowed from the pass ahead twisted through the sub–alpine environment and was always in close proximity to the trail. The path itself was in reasonable shape and nothing like the frustrating trail tread of the day before. The views were generous in all directions on that clear, sunny morning and I remember that time as one of the more pleasant hiking periods of the whole summer. We kept our binoculars trained on the surrounding ridges, hoping to see some caribou. Some hikers had, in fact, seen two of these ungulates in this vicinity the previous day. The stream added dimension and beauty to these extensive meadows and the staggered groves of Englemann spruce provided a dark green contrast to the golden glades we walked through during the morning. There still lingered some old winter snow on the northern slopes of Vertex Peak off to our left and we wondered if perhaps, in a bid to escape the heat and flies, our elusive caribou were not bedded down and chewing their cud on the cooling snow pack.

To relax on top of a pass in the mountains, on a warm, clear summer day is to feel the contentment of paradise. We sat on MacCarib Pass for over an hour, drinking in the expansive views. Here we could look back down on the far–reaching Ramparts, their craggy features diffused by smoke haze and distance. To the southeast, rising above Oldhorn Mountain, the snow–capped summit of Mount Edith Cavell curved gracefully into the heavens. We gazed down Portal Creek and across the Athabasca River valley to the Maligne and Colin Ranges, mountains that lay to the east of Jasper town. The open tundra basin nature of the pass offered wonderful sight lines in which to glass for animals and we knew, from earlier reports, that there was a sow grizzly and cub in the area, however all was still and quiet on that hot and windless afternoon.

We hiked down into the forest and arrived at the Portal creek Campground in the oppressive heat of mid–afternoon. As my hiking partner cooled her heels in the waters of the creek, I moved through the campground trying to make a decision on whether or not we should spend the night there. While we had not voiced our concerns to each other, we were both thinking of the possible presence of a mother grizzly nearby. We had the energy and time to continue on and the prospect of a campground shower was always an enticement.

I sat with my back against a tree and looked up the green slope that rose above the tenting area. On a shoulder of Peveril Peak, an avalanche fan swept down from the upper ridges to the valley bottom. These slopes quite often provide the roots, forbs and bulbs that are essential grizzly food. It seemed a little strange that Parks would locate a campground here, so close to an apparent food source. In front of my boots lay a healthy field of cow parsnip, the first sign of this plant I had seen for several days. Was this not also a bear food? Why would we knowingly set up our tent on this salad bar? While we tried to keep things in perspective and not let our imagination run amok, there were some inalienable facts. There was a grizzly here, 36 hours ago, possibly pushed off her food source by Trish and Marco. The fatal mauling here in 1992, had occurred during a year of poor berry production and early snows, by a hungry, frustrated bear. Had that bear headed back to the avalanche slopes he had frequented during the summer months in search of remnant nutrition, and become enraged by hikers blocking his food source? There was no answer, but Cecilia and I have always believed that you should never tempt fate by plonking your nylon refuge smack on the dinner plate of a bear!

I wandered back down to the creek as Cecilia was letting her feet dry on the warm sedges of the stream bank. Having lived with each other for over 30 years, we knew each other well and after a rest and some chocolate, in unspoken accord we bounced our packs up onto our shoulders for the final 9–kilometre push to the trailhead on Portal Creek The surging cacophony of the trailside stream as it hurtled to the valley floor made conversation impossible and we settled into individual thoughts of the past few days as the evening sun sank into the west and our satiated bodies sank into the forest.

The Jetta sat in the evening shade and I fumbled for the keys. I heard my partner get the Jeep started as I eased into the leather comfort of Marco's new toy. We drove up the long and winding road, as the old Beatles tune goes, to the Youth Hostel arriving just at dark. I jumped out and got our packs over to my truck as Cecilia locked up the Jeep and secreted the key away in the pre arranged spot. As Marco had an extra set of keys for the Jetta, I put his set under the floor mat and slammed the door shut. I came back a few moments later and pulled on the door handle, just to ensure that all was locked and noticed a flashing red light on the dash. A screeching howl immediately issued from under the hood of the car. I had triggered the car alarm by pulling on the door handle! I shrugged my shoulders; not much we could do about that right now, the keys were locked in the car. We were by ourselves in a parking lot in a remote area, in the dark, so we jumped in our truck and watched as the Jetta sat with lights flashing, howling at the moon as it crested the skyline ridge of Edith Cavell. I thought that it would probably shut itself down after a bit and it did precisely that, three minutes or so later. We took off down the road in our half ton and laughed out loud as we thought of Trish and Marco, coming awake in some distant campground in the Tonquin Valley and listening to the far off sound of their wailing car, echoing up from the valley below.

BIRTHDAY AT KIWETINOK LAKE

The charging plunge of Takakkaw Falls filled the valley with spray and noise on that late summer morning as we stood in the parking lot, sorting through our packs. This fabulous cascade of pounding foam and water falls 400 metres from the Waputik Icefield and Daly Glacier in Yoho National Park.

The hike would carry us into the Little Yoho Valley on a circular route that would take four days and cover about 40 kilometres. "Yoho," in the native tongue of the Stoney Indians, was a word that was used to register surprise or amazement. Though we had been through these valleys numerous times over the years, we had yet to backpack and stay overnight on these trails. This hike would take on a bit of a special flavour for us, as our daughters, Heather and Cindy, would be hiking in to meet us at one of the backcountry campgrounds. On this, my last hike of the season, I would have my entire family for company! They were coming in to share Cecilia's birthday, which we hoped to celebrate at Kiwetinok Lake. This lake sits at the base of a boulder fan at an elevation of 2450 metres, and is reputed to be the highest named lake in Canada. We had been to the lake once before, almost 30 years ago.

The initial four kilometres was a gentle forest walk along the boulder–strewn Yoho River. One usually shared this part of the trail with many day–trippers out for an afternoon stroll to Laughing Falls, which is a short and pleasing walk from the parking area. As Cecilia and I wound our way along the riverbank to the distant Twin Falls Campground, we chatted about the early history of the area.

The first exploration of the Yoho Valley was carried out in 1897, by Jean Habel, a German mathematics professor and accomplished mountaineer. His guide, packer, cook and horses were supplied by none other than the famous Tom Wilson, a man credited with the discovery of both Lake Louise and Emerald Lake. Habel was interested in finding a route by which he could scale the imposing cliffs of Mount Balfour, a mountain rising directly east of the swiftly flowing Yoho River. All previous attempts to climb Balfour had been made from the Bow Valley, farther to the east, and thus far, all attempts had failed. Nothing was known about the valley to the west of Mount Balfour, through which the Yoho River flowed. The local population of Field, had never explored the valley as the river it contained was too swift to support a fish population, and too wild to hold game animals for the Native population to hunt. The Yoho River flows into the Kicking Horse River at the entrance to this valley. The glacial till and outwash from these rivers, combined with the deadfall near the surging waters, provided an effective blockade against entry to this wild valley. If Habel wished to visit and explore the area, then another route, more suitable to horses, would have to be found.

Habel's entourage, with Ralph Edwards as guide, finally succeeded in finding a pass, about six kilometres northeast of Emerald Lake. In so doing, they discovered a small lake on the pass and named it Summit Lake, now referred to as Yoho Lake. From there they laboriously chopped a trail down through the timber to the valley of the Yoho River. After a long day, the horses and men emerged on the glacial flats under a great fall of water they named Takakkaw, a Stoney phrase meaning "It is wonderful." From there, they pressed on upstream, passing by several waterfalls, among them Point Lace, Laughing and Twin Falls. Eventually they arrived at the toe of the Yoho Glacier where the river flowed from a large ice cave. They spent several days there, walking on the glacier and trying to find a route up the steep sides of Mount Balfour, but to no avail. In rainy weather and with little provisions left, they backtracked down the Valley of the Yoho to the foot of Takakkaw Falls. It was here that the wranglers decided to push on down the river course rather than going back up over the newly discovered Yoho Pass, which would have been a great hardship for the tough little mountain ponies to negotiate. Cutting instead, through massive deadfall along the valley bottom, they eventually came out on the alluvial flats of the Kicking Horse River just east of present day Field.

When Tom Wilson queried his guide on their literally "ground breaking" experience, Ralph Edwards was very enthusiastic and waxed eloquently about the area, describing to his boss the incredible waterfalls they had seen, as well as the impressive tongue of the Yoho Glacier. Subsequently, Tom Wilson approached the Canadian Pacific Railway with the idea of building a wagon road in to Takakkaw Falls. The area, he claimed, was sure to be a major tourist attraction given its' magnificent height and scenic grandeur. CPR officials were always on the lookout for new ways of attracting tourists to the mountains who would of course use their rail line as a means of transportation. They had recently constructed a rough road to Emerald Lake, located in a picturesque valley to the west. Tally–Ho's, carriages pulled by horses, were used on this path to the lake by the guests who stayed at Mount Stephen House in Field. Acting on Tom Wilson's information, a wagon road was pushed through the valley of the Yoho River in the next few years. Later, in 1908, the CPR built a log chalet at the foot of Twin Falls, for the use of railroad clients and the burgeoning mountaineering community. Twin Falls Chalet is still in use today, the rustic structure providing a unique backcountry experience for people visiting the National Parks.

It was to Twin Falls that we were headed that warm afternoon. The Twin Falls Campground is located on the banks of a creek of the same name, a little over a kilometre away from the chalet. It was not possible to see Twin Falls from the site, however we could hear the thundering sound through the forest canopy. We made an early dinner and sat by the stream, then left in the twilight to explore to the toe of the Yoho Glacier, about three kilometres away. In the fading light we hiked along the Yoho River and ascended into the rocky chasm from which the river flowed. The sunset coated the mountains in flaming orange and the distant ice sheet of the Waputik was spread in golden splendour across the base of the peaks. We were unable to climb to the toe of the ice as nightfall was not too far away, so we contented ourselves in this lonely valley by watching the sun fade from the hills.

The Yoho Glacier is only one of several glaciers forming part of the Waputik Icefield, a vast sheet of ice that straddles the Great Divide. The word Waputik comes to us from the Stoneys and is their word for the white goat, what we refer to now as a mountain goat. Some people are confused about the difference between a glacier and an icefield. A suitable analogy might be for one to take a common, Styrofoam coffee cup, and with thumb and forefinger, pinch away little chunks from the rim. One then fills the coffee cup, or alpine basin, with soft ice cream and that becomes the "icefield". As the ice cream fills to the top of the cup, it begins to overflow the rim where the bits have been pinched off: The ice cream starts to flow down the sides and become "glaciers." In the case of the Waputik Icefield, there are at least six separate glaciers flowing from the icefield to the bordering valleys. Some of the named glaciers on this icefield include the Bow, Peyto, Yoho, Bath, Daly and Niles.

In the blue dusk of late evening we made our way back to camp to find that several other late hikers had arrived at the campground. As my summer had progressed I became quite accustomed to sharing "my" mountains with other hikers. I enjoyed the camaraderie and informal chats in camp at night. But for me, hiking is not a "team sport". Most backcountry travellers prefer to appreciate the wilderness quietly; they come to seek peace in the forest. This is not usually possible in a crowded campsite. And so, at every opportunity, I worked diligently to find quiet places in which I could be alone, to be by myself or with my wife. As the season passed, I spent no more time than necessary near the tenting areas. Robert Service once penned: "It's the beauty that fills me with wonder. It's the silence that fills me with peace." Fortunately, despite the fact there must have been 30 souls about, the camp was quiet as the inky night fell on the forest and the stars tinkled in the sky.

~

A cobalt–blue dawn greeted us as we stumbled from our nylon shelter the next morning. The sun was a dazzling brilliance on the rocky faces above, yet the forest was still in deep shadow. We sat and sipped our warm brews as the morning sun came to the forest and the camp came alive with voices and movement. We hikers certainly were a colourful bunch with our yellow tents and blue packs, our purple and orange anoraks, red gaiters and pink neckerchiefs, the glint of cameras and sunglasses, the shiny aluminium walking sticks. It seemed as if collectively, we were imploring the soft green forest and the cold grey rocks to wake up with us; come alive, come see how intense and vibrant we are!

We ate our breakfast and stowed our belongings in our packs for the 11 kilometre hike over the Whaleback Summit to our next camp in the Little Yoho Valley. Within the hour, we caught our first glimpse of Twin Falls as it crashed over the cliff above the chalet. In his book, *The Trail to the Charmed Land*, Ralph Edwards describes his first impression of the falls: "It required no discussion to select a name for this wonderfully beautiful cascade. It named itself; Twin Falls it was called there and then, and so it appears on Habel's map…"

At this early time of day a more appropriate name for this natural feature might have been *One* Falls, as there was only one stream issuing from the precipice. The volume required to generate two outflows depends on warm sun and snowmelt. As there had been little snowfall over the previous winter, there was insufficient snow pack left in the alpine basin above the falls to make two distinct waterfalls. It was yet another indication of just how dried out our mountain watershed has become in these last few arid years.

We circled in beside the falls and climbed in the hot sun to the Waterfall Valley, almost 200 metres above Twin Falls Chalet and there we rested and took in the incredible views near the cliff edge. Directly across the valley from us, Mount Balfour filled the eastern horizon, while under that massive, sat the horn shaped Trolltinder Mountain named by Jean Habel over a hundred years ago. To the north we could see the Waputik Icefield which wrapped over the Continental Divide. The alpine nature and open views of the mountain basin behind us begged for further exploration. However, it would have to be savoured another time. Reluctantly, we pushed on to the south toward the Whaleback Summit. To the west of the trail rose Whaleback Mountain, named by British mountaineer Edward Whymper, who thought the upper shale slopes of the mountain resembled a whale breaching on the ocean surface. Whymper, famous in mountain climbing circles for being the first man to climb the Matterhorn, was travelling through this area as a distinguished guest of the CPR. We have a pretty good idea of what breaching whales really look like. We have seen them many times while visiting Hawaii and it was our humble opinion that Whymper had viewed this scene through the bottom of a whiskey bottle!

The summit of the Whaleback ridge provided one of the finest views of the entire trip. We looked from the glaciated peaks of The President and Vice–President shining in the heat haze of late afternoon, to the awesome bulk of Mount Stephen rising above the Kicking Horse valley, over to the southerly vista of the sea of peaks near Lake O'Hara, and to the faraway mountain ridges above Lake Louise. The mountain ranges marched away from us, in fading shades of blue and grey and we sat in quiet contemplation for what seemed like an hour before descending steeply down an avalanche fan and into the narrow valley of the Little Yoho.

We arrived in the Little Yoho Campground later in the afternoon to vigorous hugs from our girls. Heather and Cindy had arrived a couple of hours earlier, having come up the trail from Laughing Falls. This campground, situated on the banks of the Little Yoho River was very picturesque. The camp boasted a composting toilet, one of only three I had seen that summer, while off to the side, on a avalanche fan, a refreshing source of spring fed water issued from beneath the rocky detritus. It was one of the best laid–out backcountry campgrounds of my summer.

That evening a park warden came through and I talked with her about the composting toilets which satisfied so many environmental concerns. She informed me that were made in Cremona, a small town in southern Alberta. The cost for each toilet to Parks Canada was over $30,000. They were pleasing to the nose and eye, and totally functional in a sensitive environment.

Our family chatted away the evening, catching up on each other's news until long after dark. Then we crawled into our snug tents for a well–deserved rest.

~

I was up at the crack of dawn to take in the fantastic rose–tinted clouds as the sun climbed over the Waputik Range east of camp. The girls brewed their mother a morning birthday coffee and we set about getting her ready to receive her birthday present, a three kilometre climb of over 400 metres to a freezing cold lake in an austere and rocky setting! Some folks get such fantastic gifts!

As we ascended through the rocky debris of the retreating ice sheets, we enjoyed the ever–expanding views of the President glacier. While most of the summer flowers were gone, we did notice the odd fleabane and arnica standing strong against the cool nights of early fall. We climbed up across the talus slopes, and looked back down on the Stanley Mitchell Hut, a mountaineering cabin that was built in 1941 by the Alpine Club of Canada. The bleakness of the rocky arena through which we travelled was relieved by the warm sunshine and blue sky; the stream beside us chuckled and burbled its way to the valley below.

Kiwetinok Lake was just as we had remembered it when we had last visited it 30 years ago, but to Heather and Cindy, it was a new and fresh experience and they danced over the rocks in youthful jubilation. The name for the lake, again from the Stoney language, means, "on the north side." We cut west beyond the lake to Kiwetinok Pass, and gazed into the distant Amiskiwi Valley. Whymper and his group traversed this pass for the first time in 1901. Their horse party descended the creek drainage and managed finally to return to Field. The trip had been arduous, with muskeg and fallen timber blocking most of the route. To this day, the valley of tiny Kiwetinok Creek remains a remote and seldom–visited part of Yoho National Park. I glanced down into the green forest and sarcastically wondered if Whymper had spotted any more "whales" down there! We spent over two hours on the pass, far above the trees, the scenery a visual repast for our hungry eyes.

I spent part of this time quietly observing my family drink in the scenery in varied ways, and as I watched, I understood that each one of them was garnering strength for body and soul. Cecilia, smiled contentedly. Having her family close to her in this peaceful environment was all she had ever wanted or asked for. Cindy, my younger daughter was lost in a reflective mood, and seemed to be listening intently to the blue mountain ranges out west, while Heather was scrambling to a rocky arête above our heads, the stones singing to her spirit. For me, well, my hiking summer was virtually at an end. I knew it would be a challenge to describe my adventures to people and friends back home in a way that would allow them to understand the deep feelings of enchantment, enlightenment and mysticism I experienced over the summer. Monitoring my family that day however, I had all the proof I needed that at least they would know and understand.

~

The morning of August 31 was windy and showery and it was a challenge to get breakfast made and camp packed away between the rain showers that were being thrown at us from above. We intended to hike the fabulously beautiful Iceline Trail as it wound under the Emerald Glacier on its way to the valley floor by Takakkaw Falls. The trail was built in 1987 and offers stellar views of the Yoho Valley and a close up look at the glaciated environs under The Vice–President.

We climbed up from the campground and entered the bleak and featureless boulder–strewn topography of the Iceline Trail. We left the last remnants of the forest just as a lightning storm swept in over the craggy precipices above. As we sought refuge near some rocks and scraggly spruce an enormous bolt of lightning jagged in to the boulder field opposite. The immediate resounding thunder clap rolled over and through us, and seemed to deafen us momentarily. I had actually seen the strike arc in towards us and thought that we were within 300 feet of the contact point. With six kilometres of exposed terrain ahead, the dad and husband in me questioned the choice of route considering we were carrying metal tent poles in our packs, and had aluminium hiking poles in our hands. But my companions would not be denied. Cindy in particular, had been waiting three years to hike the trail.

After the shower had passed across the valley of the Yoho River we decided to venture on, though we all kept a close eye on the summit ridge to our right, watching for the first telltale signs of the next tempest to come boiling over the summit. Gradually the sun started to peek from under the clouds and a precious rainbow materialized over the western end of the valley. We marched on over the moraine, spread out from each other a bit because of our different hiking gaits. The grey rocks and monochromatic sky turned the blues of the glacial tarns into fantastic hues of aqua marine. Our raingear, in vivid splashes of neon purple, yellow and orange provided a refreshing contrast to the wet, grey drabness of the rocky marginal moraine.

With our typical good fortune, however, the day took a turn for the better, the sun came out and all was at once fine again. "Sublime in the alpine," was the way Heather put it. We had been alone up here for several hours, the morning lightning had apparently kept most hikers away from the trail. We hiked along enjoying the diffuse light on Mount Balfour and the distant Yoho glacier as the sun sought its way out from under the heavy storm–cloud blanket. Along the way we were treated to a substantial rock fall from the serrated ridge above the trail. Great limestone boulders bounced and leaped down toward us, reducing themselves quickly from coffee–shop to coffee–table and, gradually, to coffee–cup size. The thunder of their passing and the resulting dust cloud rolled away on the light wind. As the sun burned off the remaining storm clouds, I became more relaxed, and while my spirit soared, my body descended through the damp forest to Takakkaw Falls. All at once we were down in the meadows and out from the deep shadows of the forest. I eased the pack off my shoulders and set it down, slowly and gently. I reclined into the trailside grass, took a deep breath and in that split second, my hiking summer was complete. Was it not just yesterday that I had waved good–bye to Cecilia on the trail to Egypt Lake? I looked around me as if something should be happening; what I had no clue. I looked over to my family and their warm smiles conveyed, "Way to go, dad!"

While Heather and Cindy hiked back up to the parking lot to retrieve the trucks, Cecilia and I relaxed in the flower–strewn meadow. With the muted roar of the Takakkaw Falls wafting above the pines, I contemplated the immediate future. The fact that I would be returning to my duties as a bus driver the next day was ameliorated somewhat by the knowledge that I was taking the last two weeks of September to go hiking in the larches. For part of that time, we would be visiting Shadow Lake Lodge, nestled in the forest beneath Mount Ball. It would be a time of rest and a chance to think back over the trails and passes of the last few weeks.

THE LARCHES OF SHADOW LAKE

As fall colours dressed the mountain valleys, we embarked on our last hike of the season. It was late September and after being back at work for two weeks, I was ready to get out on the trails again. We were on our way to the log-cabin ambience of Shadow Lake Lodge, 15 kilometres away. This would be a five–day trip to visit the alpine passes near the lodge and enjoy the magic that happens every year when the larch trees parade their vivid orange and yellow hues across the alplands.

The time would also provide me with a chance to reflect on my outstanding summer adventures. When I had passed through this area on my first trip of the summer, I had thought ahead to the autumn when I could just sit in a log cabin, snuggle with Cecilia and tell her tall tales of the splendid treasures I had uncovered. Now that time was at hand and I was eagerly anticipating the forthcoming days.

At the trailhead, near Red Earth Creek, a Parks Canada warning stapled to a tree offered an ominous beginning to our trek; a vast amount of the trail system was closed because of the presence of an aggressive grizzly bear. An area to the south of the lodge, including Whistling Pass, Egypt Lakes and Healy Pass carried a bear warning, while the area to the north, encompassing Gibbon Pass, Twin Lakes and Arnica Lake was closed outright, to hikers. Virtually the entire trail I had hiked in July was presently closed to back country travellers.

Grizzlies are extremely active at this time of year as they bulk up against the onslaught of winter. They forage extensively and continually, ingesting everything within reach. They become anxious and stressed as their bodies crave more protein and fat–producing nutrients; as a result, they are easy to aggravate. Park Wardens usually advise hikers to always travel in groups of four or more, and make lots of noise during the fall season.

We set off up the trail shortly before noon in a misty rain. The cool temperature was invigorating after the intense heat of the summer. The frost had nipped the understory plants and their bright splashes of red, orange and gold provided a refreshing contrast to the drab forest and overcast skies. We walked along the trail for two hours before crossing Red Earth Creek to the campground at Lost Horse Creek. The trail we were on was part of the old tote road coming down from the mine at Talc Lake. Mining was concluded in that area about 55 years ago; however, up until recently, the track had been kept in good repair and was used by the warden service for fire protection. The old road is currently in a state of natural regeneration with grasses and shrubs filling the ruts and is now only used by hikers, mountain bikers, and pack horses that bring supplies in to the lodge at Shadow Lake. We arrived in mid afternoon and were greeted with hot tea and biscuits before being shown to our cabin. These cabins have names that reflect area features such as Egypt, Healy, Ball, Red Earth, Sphinx, Pilot, Storm and Shadow. Our cabin was called Whistling, and was named after the nearby alpine pass.

The cabins and lodge are tucked in the forest on the fringe of a broad meadow, about one kilometre away from the lake. Originally built by the CPR in 1928, it was bought by Brewster Transport around 1940 and kept in the Brewster family until just a few years ago. While the cabins have no running water, they are supplied with propane heat and heavy down duvets. All the guests take their meals in a large, log dining facility and the original building, constructed with local logs over 80 years ago, serves as a common sitting–reading room, complete with soft sofas, throw rugs on a hardwood floor and a cheery fireplace.

We met with some other guests over dinner that evening and then, in the gathering gloom, we repaired to our cabin to play some cards. The kerosene lamps threw warm shadows on the log walls and we relaxed in these quiet surroundings as the showers continued. During the night we were awakened by driving rain and ear splitting thunder that crashed across the valley floor. The attendant lightning display was dramatic as it lit the meadowland in front of the cabin and jagged along the mountain ridgelines.

~

The grey light of dawn brought with it the chilly spectre of fresh snow that draped the peaks from summit to well below the tree line. As was the daily custom of the lodge staff, a soft knocking on the door at 7:30 am indicated the arrival of a basin of hot water for our morning ablutions. The dinner bell rang precisely at 8 am and as we trundled on down the path to the awaiting hot coffee, we could see our breath in the still morning air. Pancakes and porridge, fresh fruit with berries and yogurt put the guests, of which there were nine, in high spirits.

The staff at the lodge happily informed us that the wardens were not concerned about the trail closures, as long as we hiked in groups. Some of the guests was outbound that day, while another couple was going up to the lake. Cecilia and I were here principally for the larches and as today was cloudy and cool, we decided to rest and read, and hope for better weather to move into the valley. To climb up to the alpine and wander through the splendid larches in their fall foliage on a clear day with a sapphire–blue sky is something most hikers can never forget.

The restful nature of the lodge induced a quiet lethargy, and we were very content to just sit by the fire on this grey dismal day and soak in some local history in the confines of this historic lodge. Another reason for coming in to Shadow Lake was to peruse their extensive library for research purposes. I had noticed, as I passed through here in July, the old books in the CPR cabin, and thought I would avail myself of them when I returned in the fall. It was just the kind of day to do that and the hours sped by in companionable silence. The three people on staff were busy with their chores and we were left to ourselves; we did not see a soul until early evening when Russ and Andrea, two recent arrivals, came by to introduce themselves.

That evening, as darkness closed in on our snug retreat, I ambled back down to the CPR cabin to do some more research and writing. The soft light of the kerosene lamps flickering through the windows of the little cabins provided a tenuous warmth as

I moved through the dark, wet forest to the main lodge. It was inky black and very quiet, no one was about and I had the cabin to myself. I stoked up the fire with dry, seasoned wood, and with the lamplight playing off the burnished timbers, I was quickly transported into yesteryear.

I lost all track of time and, with the rain pattering on the shingled roof, I sipped away on my fortifying flask of rye and sambuca and penned some prose. Presently, I became aware of the ethereal smell of distant pipe smoke and the faint aroma of tanned rawhide from an earlier era. I thought about tending to the fire when, all of a sudden the fire grate was thrown open, and a chunk of tamarack was tossed in amidst a shower of sparks. "Snappin' sheepshit, where'd *you* come from?" I was startled as I hadn't even heard the door open. The apparition turned toward me and I was staring into the grizzled visage of my old pal, Bill Peyto. I sat in bewilderment and unconsciously groped for my jug, only to find it overturned and empty on the rough–hewn bench. "Damn it!" I thought. "If ever I'd needed a snort, it was now." I looked down onto the floor to see how much had spilt but to my surprise, the floor was totally dry. With a questioning frown I looked across at Bill, who was easing himself into an old leather chair. His icy blue eyes sparkled with amusement as he wiped the last dregs of my flask from his handlebar moustache. "Why now, that's right fine fixin's you got there boy. Don't remember no sambuca in my day." I sat there, speechless, and looked forlornly at the empty flask. Eventually I found my voice.

"Evenin' Bill, haven't seen you about for awhile."

"Uh, huh." He intoned.

"I'm just doing some research, I might write all this stuff up."

"Them's jes words boy. Best ya see things fer yerself," was his rejoinder.

"Yeah, I know, but its history, man, I'm interested in what went on back here in my mountains a hundred years ago."

"Still jes words son," he retorted. "I wouldn't take no great stock in 'em."

"Yeah, but Bill, there's hardly no oldtimers left around here anymore. Why I have to rely on historical records." Bill dismissed that opinion with a shrug and a wave of his gnarled old hand. There was a pause.

"I'm thinkin' you had a mighty fine summer up here." he ventured.

"Yeah Bill, I really had myself a time."

"Member when we wuz up on them ramparts a few months back and you wuz whinin' and carryin' on 'bout yer cancer?" I got kind of beady eyed; I took umbrage with his tone and brash mannerisms but hell, it was Bill; that's just the way he was. I sort of nodded.

"Wal," he sniffed. "Looks like somebody give ya' nuther shot, eh? A chance to see all this purty country you was too chickenshit to see earlier, back when you wuz young n' spry!" I grudgingly had to admit to that.

"But how'd you know where I hiked this season, Bill? I never saw you anywhere around." I had thought of him many times over the summer as I passed through some of his old stomping grounds. He pushed his stetson up on his forehead and began the slow, determined search for his pipe.

"Why hell, I bin in yer hip pocket son, right from the git, go. Why I seen ya' readin' ole' lady Schäffer's book in your camp up at Maligne, when you was up there on your canoe trip. Your fine lady liked that okay, you rattlin' on 'bout Shäffer's first visit to that lake. Later on down the trail a piece, I sure had me a good laugh when I seen ya bouncin' around in yer tent the night that rock avalanche come down on Twin Lake, and that goat thing up on Gibbon's." Bill slapped his knee and barked, "Hell, you sure was some pilgrim! Looked like it was your first time back in the woods, the way ya got all knotted up! It was just a damn goat for cripe's sake, weren't no bear!"

Bill laughed and shook his head and his icy blue eyes seemed to bore right through me. He got up and started pacing the floor; I had the feeling he was not completly comfortable in the close quarters of a cabin. He took off his hat and scratched his head as he recalled, "Ya know, I seen that bear up at Citadel long afore you guys, but you boys played 'er smart, an' moved away lickedy split." He grinned as he thought back. "Sure did like sashayin' back over t'wards Marvel with ya, ain't seen that country since me an' Wilcox wuz there in '95." He glanced in my direction with a stony squint. "That's *1895*, you young whippersnapper!" Then he chuckled, "Ha, thought yer eyes was gonna bug plumb outta yer head when you seen them clods of dirt floatin' in Cabin Lake.

You guys never did lay eyes on him, but jumpin' lord lightin' that wuz one big sumabitch of a bear!" Bill paused and looked into the fire, and quietly intoned, "I was there with you son, the day we hit the park gates in the truck and yer missus told ya about your pal gettin' took by the cancer." I thought I detected a bit of a catch in his voice. "Kind of hits a little close to home, don't it?" was all he choked out. "Then there wuz the day I seen ya' jumpin' an' ki–ying about like a snake–bit Indun when ya looked to the top of ole' Robson. Ya damn near bounced me right outta that hip pocket. Cripes, but you was happy that day! And them bugs in the Tonquin, they sure put the run on you two, eh? But that's the way of it back there son. Still worth the price, right?" Bill eased back down into his chair, "Me 'an somma the boys, we wuz the ones that played that lightnin' strike on ya, up on the Iceline."

"Shit sakes, Bill, that scared the hell out of me," I hollered. "I had to look out for my family, why did you have to go and do such a thing?"

Bill stared out the window for a moment or two and pensively tugged on his mustache, "I jes' wanted to remind ya 'bout how important yer family was to ya. See, it 'pears to this old hoss that you are some lucky to have three damn fine ladies watchin' out fer yer back, takin' care of you, even though you are a horse's ass from time to time!" I judged Bill Peyto to be the grand master of the double edged compliment. With this guy you never knew whether to extend your hand in friendship or bunch your fist in anger; jeez what a character!

"Listen son, we need to clear the air here." He hunched forward in his chair as he pawed into his shirt, bringing forth his pipe. With a practiced gesture he set about tamping the fixings in the bowl.

"If you write this stuff up," he poked the pipe stem in my direction, "by God you better get it right! Them books you been cipherin', them accounts you been pourin' over," he shook his head emphatically, "they flat out aren't the gospel truth! Sometimes they miss the mark, if ya know whata mean. You gotta remember that them guys like Hector, Coleman, Wheeler," he stopped and scratched a match to flame, "Wilcox, Porter," the bowl of his pipe came alive with a warm glow, "Habel, Mrs. Schäffer, the whole damn works of 'em, guys like me and Tom Wilson too, hell, we never did discover nothin! Sure we done some explorin' and some of us climbed up on some mountains. We did a little mappin' and surveyin' maybe, but "discoverin." Bill shook his head. "No, we didn't do none a that! Induns is the real folks should get their dues for findin' these wild places. Them's the ones took that pompous bag a' wind George Simpson, through the passes and on out to the coast. Ya think he'd a figured his own way through that blow down timber, hah!" He spat across the room. "Samson Beaver now, he drew that map for Schäffer out of nothin' but a piece of hide and some charcoal from the fire. Give it to her to take in to find her lake. The Induns took Wilson up to that lake they now call Lake Louise. Coleman would still be stumblin' around in the woods iffin old Adolphus Moberly hadn't set 'im straight! We'd a never figured out where half this shit was if we hadn't followed them ole' Indun trails. You make damn certain you don't stick these fancy pants from the city up on their high horses with all their discoveries an' pattin' each other on the back. Induns son, Induns is what really found this place!"

Bill stood up and placed his stetson back on his head. He checked to make sure his pipe was going strong and took a long, lingering glance at the empty sambuca jar. "Don't s'pose ya got anymore that snakebite left?" I shook my head and he nodded. "Prob'ly just as well. You're gonna be steppin' pretty lively around yer missus when she sees that empty crock," he chuckled. He opened the door and turned back, taking the pipe out from between his tobacco–stained teeth. Jabbing it in my direction, he said, "Ya did good son. You got strong spirit now. I kin see it. Ya hold real tight to them memories, cuz later on down the trail you'll see. See how all the damn fine times just seem to vanish, like campfire smoke when it drifts off through the forest. And the bad times, why they always seem to hang around, just a brewin' down there in the coals. Sort of the same with people I 'spect, friends come and friends go, but enemies, they accumulate. Set them good times right next to yer heart an' fight like a wolverine to keep 'em, cuz by God, they belong to you," He then winked and pointed over towards the fire. "An' don't you *never* let the fire die down." He turned, and like a wraith, was through the doorway in a heartbeat. I stood to close the door against the night chill. "Safe trails to you Bill," I whispered to the dark forest. I knew I would not see him again.

The next morning was grey and showery and after a warm wash, we went down to the dining lodge to take our breakfast with Russ and Andrea. Bacon and eggs and French toast, fresh fruit and pails of coffee filled our empty stomachs and we discussed possible trails to hike that day. Russ and Andrea were from Washington state and more than a little concerned about the possibility of crossing paths with a bear. We suggested the four of us wander up to Gibbon Pass and they readily agreed. An hour later we stepped out of the cabin and went over to the trail, ducking under the plastic taping placed there by the warden indicating the trail closure. We ascended into the alpine and within the hour we were tramping through fresh snow on the pass. The views were minimal, yet I was happy to return and show my wife the area in which I had seen my "adrenaline goat." We tried to get as much as we could out of the beautiful larches, but with the snow–laden branches and overcast skies, it was a bit of a stretch to really appreciate them. As we descended into the trees, a snow squall hit and pushed us down into the forest.

That afternoon, the two of us walked through the trees to the shores of Shadow Lake. Cecilia had not seen this particular piece of alpine beauty before. There was a strong, cold wind dusting off the lake and we stayed only a short time. The rest of the day was spent in blissful appreciation of the warmth generated by our cabin; it certainly would have been rough camping out in my tent in this weather!

~

The following day, we hiked back down to the truck. We diverted briefly to a side trail to explore the junction of Pharaoh and Red Earth creeks. There was a warden patrol cabin there and we walked around the corral, tool shed and cabin. The last time I was here had been in 1972, and it was interesting to see the area again. The two streams were flowing clear and icy cold with the coming fall, and yellow aspen leaves twirled and floated along on the surface. We wandered slowly back down the valley of the Red Earth, each of us lost in introspection.

I mused that I had enjoyed an inspiring summer. I had hiked up and over 17 passes and gazed into distant, far–reaching valleys. I had seen at least 65 backcountry lakes and alpine tarns, every single one of them a pristine jewel of incredible colour, containing a thousand shimmering memories.

I had hiked close to 450 kilometres in four National and two Provincial parks. During my days out I had seen six goats, about a dozen bighorn Rams, four deer, 4 moose including a cow moose with twin calves, 2 elk and a grizzly bear. It had been a healing journey of the heart and of the body, and an incredible voyage of discovery, wherein I was able to redefine my inner strength and resolve.

Yesterday is history,
tomorrow is a mystery.
Today is a *gift*,
that's why they call it....
the *present*.

Elevation Index of Mountains

Alcantara	3021	(9911)
Aquila	2880	(9446)
Assiniboine	3617	(11870)
Aye	3243	(10639)
Baker	3172	(10407)
Balfour	3273	(10741)
Ball	3306	(10847)
Barbette	3048	(10000)
Blackhorn	3001	(9840)
Boomerang	2834	(9300)
Brachiopod	2651	(8695)
Brussilof	3045	(9990)
Cautley	2870	(9418)
Cavell	3363	(11033)
Citadel	2608	(8556)
Chak	2798	(9179)
Clitheroe	2749	(9020)
Douglas	3357	(11017)
Drysdale	2932	(9620)
Eon	3310	(10857)
Fossil	2946	(9663)
Foster	3204	(10512)
Geikie	3308	(10854)
Gray	3000	(9843)
Grindl	2773	(9105)
Haiduk	2919	(9578)
Helmet	3401	(11160)
Kiwetinok	2902	(9518)
Limestone	2878	(9443)
Lynx	3191	(10471)
Magog	3094	(10150)
Mistaya	3078	(10100)
Monarch	2903	(9525)
Mumm	2962	(9718)
Nexus	2834	(9300)
Nub	2743	(8999)
Numa	2550	(8367)
Og	2874	(9429)
Oldhorn	2986	(9797)
Oyster	2777	(9108)
Parapet	3018	(9905)

Peveril	2679	(8790)
Pharaoh	2710	(8892)
Pika	3033	(9950)
President	3138	(10293)
Ptarmigan	3059	(10033)
Quartz Hill	2580	(8464)
Rearguard	2743	(9002)
Redoubt	2902	(9518)
Richardson	3086	(10122)
Robson	3953	(12972)
Skoki	2696	(8845)
St. Bride	3315	(10875)
Storm	3161	(10372)
Strom	3024	(9921)
Terrapin	2944	(9658)
Throne	3120	(10234)
Towers	2846	(9337)
Vice President	3066	(10057)
Whitehorn	3392	(11130)
Wonder	2850	(9350)

ELEVATION INDEX OF PASSES

Boulder	2345	(7694)
Citadel	2360	(7742)
Gibbon	2286	(7500)
Healy	2315	(7595)
Jones	2210	(7250)
Kiwetinok	2480	(8136)
Limestone	2170	(7120)
MacCarib	2180	(7150)
Marvel	2200	(7217)
Numa	2355	(7726)
Packer's	2495	(8185)
Robson	1649	(5410)
Rockwall	2240	(7249)
Tumbling	2250	(7381)
Whistling	2271	(7451)
Wolverine	2210	(7250)
Wonder	2395	(7858)

A Selected Bibliography

Beers, Don. *Banff-Assiniboine: A Beautiful World*. Calgary: Highline Publishing, 1993.

Beers, Don. *The World of Lake Louise*. Calgary: Highline Publishing, 1991.

Beers, Don. *Jasper-Robson: A Taste of Heaven*. Calgary: Highline Publishing, 1996.

Brewster, F. O. "Pat". *Weathered Wood*. Banff: Self published, 1977.

Camp, Frank. *Roots in the Rockies*. Ucluelet: Frank Camp Ventures, 1993.

Deegan, Jim & Porter John. *Timberline Tales*. Banff: Peter Whyte Foundation, 1977.

Edwards, Ralph. *The Trail to the Charmed Land*. Saskatoon: H. R. Larson Publishing, 1950.

Fraser, Esther. *The Canadian Rockies*. Calgary: Fifth House, 2002.

Fraser, Esther. *Wheeler*. Banff: Summerthought, 1978.

Gadd, Ben. *Handbook of the Canadian Rockies*. Jasper: Corax Press, 1995.

Gest, Lillian. *History of Mt. Assiniboine*. Self published, 1979.

Holgrem, Eric. *Place Names in Alberta*. Edmonton: Self published, 1973.

Hart, E. J. Ain't it Hell. *Bill Peyto's Mountain Journal*. Banff: E. J. H. Literary Enterprises, 1995.

Hart, E. J. *Diamond Hitch*. Banff: Summerthought, 1979.

Jones, Andrew. *Guardians of the High Wilderness*. Reader's Digest

Kain, Conrad. *Where the Clouds Can Go*. New York: American Alpine Club, 1935.

Luxton, Eleanor. *Banff, Canada's First National Park*. Banff: 1975.

Manry, Kathryn. Skoki. *Beyond the Passes*. Calgary: Rocky Mountain Books, 2001.

Nisbet, Jack. *Sources of the River*. 1994.

Oltmann, Ruth. *Lizzie Rummel, Baroness of the Canadian Rockies*. Calgary: Rocky Mountain Books, 1983.

Pole, Graeme. *Classic Hikes in the Canadian Rockies*. Canmore: Altitude Publishing, 1994.

Patton, Brian, Robinson, Bart. *The Canadian Rockies Trail Guide*. Banff: Summerthought, 1971.

Spry, Irene. *The Palliser Expedition*. Calgary: Fifth House, 1963.

Strom, Erling. *Pioneers on Skis*. New York: Smith Clove Press, 1977.

Tetarenko, Kim & Lorne. *Ken Jones, Mountain Man*. Calgary: Rocky Mountain Books, 1996.

Thorington, J. M. *Climbers Guide to the Rocky Mountains of Canada*. New York: American Alpine Club, 1966.

Taylor, William C. *Tracks Across My Trail*. Jasper: Jasper-Yellowhead Historical Society, 1984.

Whyte, Jon. *Rocky Mountain Madness*. 1982